VISUAL CULTURES AS

TIME TRAVEL

VISUAL CULTURES AS
TIME TRAVEL

HENRIETTE GUNKEL
AYESHA HAMEED

Sternberg Press

VISUAL CULTURES AS ... SERIES INTRODUCTION

JORELLA ANDREWS

Visual culture emerged in the mid-1990s as a new—or, rather, a newly articulated—field of inquiry that attempted to reintegrate a wide range of visual, artistic, philosophical, cultural, and political concerns. Cross-disciplinary in nature, it has become a site of encounter for divergent perspectives, including competing attitudes toward the ethical status and ideological functioning of the visual itself. Emerging from interactions between scholars, artists, curators, and activists, visual culture has also encouraged multilayered, often hybrid, modes of investigation. These have done much to extend, even reposition, intellectual research beyond the traditional parameters of the university.

Given visual culture's highly differentiated character, this series of short coauthored books is not intended to be a comprehensive collection of representative texts. Indeed, its starting point—in the Visual Cultures department at Goldsmiths, University of London—was a discussion about our own diverse investments in this still-evolving field. Each publication, therefore, invites a multifaceted investigation of a single, pertinent topic. In each case, two colleagues with shared interests—and differing points of view—examine their chosen subject in a particularized and probing manner. The format is always the same: two essays and a conversation. But within this scheme, contents unfold in their own way with respect to their positions, polemics, and poetics. In some instances, it has been appropriate to combine newly commissioned work with essays that were written some time ago, or with material that has existed, until now, in lecture form only. The conversations, staged for the purpose of these volumes, provide fruitful context and offer a first layer of reflection and response in what are emphatically open and ongoing debates.

VISUAL CULTURES AS TIME TRAVEL

A CONVERSATION BETWEEN
AYESHA HAMEED AND HENRIETTE GUNKEL

9

SEA CHANGES AND OTHER FUTURISMS

AYESHA HAMEED

25

ALIEN TIME: BEING IN VERTIGO

HENRIETTE GUNKEL

59

BIBLIOGRAPHY

82

ACKNOWLEDGMENTS

86

BIOGRAPHIES

87

VISUAL CULTURES AS TIME TRAVEL

A CONVERSATION BETWEEN
AYESHA HAMEED AND HENRIETTE GUNKEL

AH Maybe we should start our conversation with what brought us to this project and to the strange conjunction of the visual (a spatial trope) and time travel (a skewing of the temporal). It is interesting that this book is coming out a few years after *Futures and Fictions*, the volume you and I coedited with Simon O'Sullivan, as the idea for this book was born around the same time or even a bit earlier.[1] *Futures and Fictions* was an exploration of what is made possible by the conjunction of the terms "futures" and "fictions" in considering the racialization of the foreclosure of the future, and this conjunction's ability to provide alternate pathways and possibilities into the real, and for me (always), the spatialization and sedimentations sparked by turning the temporal against its own grain. In a sense, then, *Visual Cultures as Time Travel* draws from *Futures and Fictions*, precedes it, follows it, undoes some of it, and reiterates a strange kind of time travel in its own right.

But what does it mean to posit visual cultures as a kind of time travel? This conjunction, when we coined it, triggered for me a kind of giddiness, a sense of absurdity and possibility. Although an ellipsis is intrinsic to the concept of the Visual Cultures as… book series as a whole, where our book is concerned, I think this implied ellipsis intensifies our title's speculative conjunction, points to the breakages and gaps between the terms, yet also posits an absurd, hopeful "what if" that is exacerbated by another set of breakages, gaps, and speculations embedded in the image of time travel. And indeed, the term "visual cultures," a proposition that unseats a disciplinary notion of the visual and the aesthetic, does not help to ground this speculative combination at all. And so (I hope!) the combination of visual cultures and time travel is a proposition that can set us tumbling through outer space and into history, trying to make sense of this journey and create narrative methods with which to mark it. Because, as in *Futures and Fictions*, we are trying to consider the visual outside of the realm of art and perhaps more in terms of witnessing and listening, and we are thinking of time travel as marked by possibility and loss in the aftermath of transatlantic slavery, and in the moment of mass illegalized migration, of blackness and time, of wildfires and floods, of lost and co-opted futures, of deep geologic time, and of falling. A sense of vertigo, falling, and disorientation that marks our present.

HG I like the way you consider the process of putting this book together as a form of time travel in its own right! And maybe I can start off with some introductory words to my contribution to this volume, as it relates to some of the aspects you just highlighted, before moving to some general thoughts on time travel. My chapter is part of a larger research project called *Alien Time*, which brings together Africanist science-fictional interventions, queer temporalities, deep space-time, and deep geologic time. I borrow the concept of alien time from Octavia E. Butler, who uses it in her novel *Kindred*, first published in 1979, to describe the very different sense of time experienced by the main protagonist as she involuntarily time travels, again and again, into her own ancestral past—a past that takes place on a plantation not unlike the one that you describe in your essay. I explore Butler's work in conversation with the artist Kitso Lynn Lelliott's multimedia project *South Atlantic Hauntings* (2013–ongoing). In both works, the temporal movement into different periods of time suggests a nonnormative approach to seeing and experiencing the world. My contribution begins with an analysis of how *Kindred* presents the possibility of thinking through the notion of time travel differently than what is on offer in mainstream science fiction, whether in cinema or literature. Neither of us seems to be very interested in conventional time-travel narratives or imageries that rely on futuristic high-tech, high-speed machinic devices that enable traveling through time (and sometimes space) in the first place, whether into a distant past or a distant future. Butler's narrative turns our attention instead to the body—or more specifically, the racialized Black body—as the technological device for time travel, which raises questions about what counts as technology and how it operates in relation to time. This is what her writing has in common with other Afrofuturist approaches—which you recently contextualized as setting out "to see the afterlife of the middle passage in a futuristic scenario."[2] This is a very different approach to the idea of leaving the past behind in an accelerated turn toward the future, as articulated, for example, in Marinetti's Futurist manifesto (1909) or Marx and Engels's *Communist Manifesto* (1848), and hints toward our common disinterest, I would say, in neatly distinguishable temporalities between which one can travel.

AH My point of entry into this reading of time travel comes from a long-term project called *Black Atlantis*, which tries to read notions of Afrofuturism with the Anthropocene. It has taken on different iterations, working through the body, through dance floors, and quite often through the ideas and music of Drexciya, a Detroit-based techno group active in the 1990s and early 2000s, who created an Afrofuturist mythos around the enslaved thrown overboard during the Middle Passage adapting to life underwater, whose fetuses adapted from living in amniotic fluid to living in seawater. My contribution here, "Sea Changes and Other Futurisms," builds on previous work in the form of a live audiovisual essay I made on the concept of the Plantationocene. In 2017, during a visit I made to a former sugar plantation in Barbados, I tried to read the different temporal registers of the histories of plantations. I was also thinking about the improbable temporal scale of the Plantationocene, which views the plantation as the first machine to have produced capitalism as we know it, a machine that efficiently instrumentalizes both bodies and territories. The essay in this book intermixes that visit I made to Barbados with visits to Trinidad and to a small island called Seili in the Finnish archipelago. I use my trip to Seili as a point of entry into thinking about time on two registers: horizontal time and vertical time.

It is interesting that there's a spatial turn in both of our bodies of work. Mine quite literally looks at notions of territory, whether seascapes or landscapes, while in your work, space appears in your description of dizziness, vertigo, and the sense of falling. This is manifest in your discussion of several works, including *Kindred* and a text by the American dramatist, filmmaker, and critic Frank B. Wilderson III.

Another idea that I wanted to bring up is the notion of the time series, which figures in my essay as a particular model for horizontal time, and how this might relate to the notion of horizon, which is an important term in both of our essays.

HG You are right, one of my main foci in this contribution is the sense of free fall and vertigo (which both involve a loss of horizon), although in my reading of Lelliott's work, I am also thinking about deep space-time and the different types of bodies—human, machine, planetary, spectral, ancestral—that inhabit the sky.

The sense of vertigo that I try to conceptualize in relation to the history of slavery and colonialism and its afterlives has also been increasingly theorized as the general condition of the aftermath of the 2007–8 financial crash, in which the lack of a horizon produced a destabilized sense of being in the world as well as the disappearance of a linear notion of time and its view onto a calculable future[3]—something that we might also link to phenomena such as the escalating mental health crisis we are witnessing among students and staff at Goldsmiths and elsewhere in higher education.

The time series is interesting because, at first sight, it seems only to offer a predictive timeline laid out toward a calculable future. You describe encountering algae tanks with different levels of salinity in the laboratory in Seili, which seem to materialize a predictive timeline of gradual change. Therefore, it seems to be not a question of *if* this will happen but rather a question of *when*. Each tank, then, provides what you call a slice of time and forms a connection with the tank that precedes it and the one that follows (with a presumed higher level of salinity)—a predictive model that seems to suggest that we will gradually move from one condition to the next as we move from one tank to the next. But such an understanding of horizontal time would strengthen the horizon rather than unsettle it. What you are proposing is more complex: the tanks that are laid out in a series may or may not translate into a timeline. As you argue in your essay, "Each tank, then, is a model of a possible future state of the sea," which means it is far less predictable—and so is the sense of horizon. The "slice of time" that each tank proffers as a possible future of the Baltic Sea—and of the lives within it—is placed in a series that may or may not provide an order of temporal and spatial connections. In your argument, the horizon as a stable perspective onto the future is unsettled.

AH I'd like to stay at the surface of the water for now, because I think the depths of the sea raise another set of issues that I hope we can take on later in this conversation. I think my notion of horizontal time ties in literally with your concept of the horizon. The horizon comes into play even when thinking about the disappearing and reappearing islands that I mention in "Sea Changes." If you think of the ocean under the conditions of the Anthropocene as increasingly covering more of the planet's surface, it's clear we are becoming more maritime. Where is the horizon in relation to the islands that cultural historian Dilip Menon describes as disappearing and reappearing? Rising sea levels and the accompanying loss of vantage points that were once provided by these islands highlight the shifting sense of what a horizon might be, and its instability as a concept.

As you indicated earlier, another interesting idea in your essay is that Butler does not use a traditional notion of time travel. In *Kindred* there is no time machine (unlike in H. G. Wells's novel, which you also mention in your text). Butler does not describe a spatiotemporal mode of travel; Dana is in one space, and then isn't—a phenomenon she tries to deal with in a pragmatic way. Her response is more like: Oh, I'm here, so now what am I going to do? Her partner, Kevin, ties a drawstring bag around her waist filled with tools and provisions in case she spontaneously travels into the past.

You use the term "montage" to describe this kind of time travel. I think it's significant that you use filmic language; you are drawing on the visual to describe a kind of temporal shift. You use this approach elsewhere as well. It is interesting to think about how that kind of jump or cut relates to the cuts in a time series. The desire of the time series is to present its subject matter sequentially and continuously. What I try to show is that putting that order out of joint produces something else that is both spatial and temporal.

HG Absolutely. There is a graphic novel adaptation of *Kindred* out now that emphasizes my argument even more; in it, the different space-times are captured and positioned next to each other as frames that could also be seen as cinematic frames.[4] However, I would argue that the sense of montage is already evident in Butler's writing, which is quite visual. There are other examples of art practices that point to the capacity of visual culture to unsettle our sense of being in time, and hence enable a sense—or theory—of time travel.

Your discussion of the time series is very intriguing and made me think about the temporal capacity of photography, which is often understood as a slice of time. In the live audiovisual version of your essay, you capture the time series in photographic images and provide a visual mapping of the different sites you encounter. Photography, like film, has a privileged relation to time, but each has a different sense of temporality. In contrast to film, the photograph is often discussed as merely preserving the moment in which the image was taken, authenticating what "has been," as Roland Barthes put it, and thus inscribing an understanding of reality into its representation of the past. The photograph is therefore discussed foremost in relation to immobility and stillness, which points to the image's perceived inability to unfold over time (the single image as opposed to the filmstrip). While movement tends to assert the presence of a continuous "now," stillness (which is not the same as lack of duration) brings a resonance of "then" to the surface, which seems to suggest photography's relationship to the present (the moment when I *see* the photograph representing what has been) but without any sense of futurity. This is why several theorists, including Barthes and Ariella Azoulay, have conceptualized photography in relation to nonchronological time.[5]

In their capacity to produce a nonchronological sense of time, photography and your time series via the tanks become very interesting in ways that may link back to your discussion of the horizon. The shot itself does not move, but a sequence of shots implies movement abstractly (and this is where montage also comes in, I think). The photograph—as with the tanks you describe and capture—waits for connections in order to create a sense of movement and thus (chronological?) time. These connections become visible through the images included in the live audiovisual version of your essay (and, in a more limited sense, in this published version) in relation to each other.

AH I'm thinking about this idea of montage and stretching, because elsewhere you talk about stretching and slowing down time. This reminds me of

Andrei Tarkovsky's description of time pressure within a film sequence, where he explains that as a shot gets longer and longer we feel the pressure of time.[6] I think there is a kind of filmic aspect to your essay.

I think this idea of montage gets thickened in both of our pieces. This happens in your essay when you talk about the time slip as a kind of haunting and doubling. In my essay, this thickening is manifest in my discussion of Nicholas Mirzoeff's concept of revolutionary time. He describes how, in New Orleans, there is an ancestral, spiritual belief that the hurricanes befalling them are acts of the gods in recapitulation of or retribution for the transportation of the enslaved across the Atlantic. Therefore, the question he raises is this: Why are the descendants of once enslaved people the ones now being killed?

This is where he describes a notion of revolutionary time in the wake of transatlantic slavery as a pulling of bodies back into the sea, toward the west coast of Africa. It's not a force of justice; rather, it's a force of retribution. It pulls bodies back to where they belong, and where they belong, according to this narrative, is in the sea. And so he sees revolutionary time as the juxtaposition of two historical moments: the Middle Passage, and the recent hurricanes in the Caribbean and southern United States. These storms in the present form a supercurrent to the undercurrent that centuries earlier had pulled the ships westward across the Atlantic. So, these two moments form a kind of montage as well, which I think also ties in with the idea of haunting and the time slip that your essay talks about.

HG This sense of revolutionary time that you describe in relation to Mirzoeff is most powerful, and in fact the hurricane—the supercurrent, as you call it—recalls the nauseating loss of balance that is central to the very conceptualization of vertigo. It offers us an understanding of the sea beyond the surface, as it opens up to a vertical world of volume that your long-term project *Black Atlantis* has so convincingly drawn attention to.

Our late colleague Mark Fisher talks about "the looped time of Afrofuturist trauma" in his essay on hauntology and Afrofuturism, where he also discusses Butler's *Kindred.* He writes: "The deep, unbearable ache in *Kindred* arises from the horrible realisation that, for contemporary black America, to wish for the erasure of slavery is to call for the erasure of itself. What to do if the precondition of your being is the abduction, murder and rape of your ancestors?"[7] I first understood the time travel that we see operating in *Kindred* as a hauntological form of time travel, but I think we need to distinguish between spectral time—the haunting of another time that is very much in the here and now, coexisting in the now—and the time travel we encounter in *Kindred*, where a movement in time and space takes place. My friend Sam Nightingale posed a question that I find significant to raise here: If movement is required to access these different periods of time, do you think this could still privilege a linear notion of time that is imbued with the notion of historical progress?

AH We thought we could usefully bring two video works into our conversation to address the question of the loss of horizon and to consider processes of verticality and vertical time. The first is a video installation by Sondra Perry called *Typhoon coming on* (2018). Its title references J. M. W. Turner's *Slavers Throwing Overboard the Dead and Dying, Typhoon Coming On* (1840), aspects of which were also rendered by Perry onto the entirety of the Serpentine Sackler Gallery's interior walls.

In one of two rooms in the Serpentine Sackler was a video about surveillance, and projected onto the wall behind it was a magnification of the surface of Perry's own skin. When seated, if you looked to the left and to the right, you saw images of waves through the door frames. In an interview, Perry describes how, when she was commissioned to make this installation, she actually wanted to wrap the entire gallery with projections of her skin. But then her curator suggested wrapping the gallery in water instead. Perry thought that this was a good suggestion in the context of this project, because if water is surrounding the space, representations of the body are no longer required—you, the viewer, become the body in this space.[8] Significantly, this particular sense of watery embodiment resonates with Christina Sharpe's uncanny notion of residence time, through which she considers the deaths of the enslaved during the Middle Passage in conjunction with the fact that bodies take 250 million years to dissolve in seawater. We both discuss this concept in our essays.

I think that this is interesting in terms of the discussion in your essay of the loss of horizon in Turner's painting, because the first thing that is lost in Perry's video is a sense of perspective. In the video, there is a disorienting sense of the camera panning up and down, or of the images themselves shifting up and down.

The bodies of the enslaved in the corner of Turner's painting are blended into the water: you see their body parts only indistinctly, so they become part of the force of the sea. As a result, the bodies are only intelligible through the storm that has been imagined onto this scene. But there is also a kind of indeterminacy, which I think resonates with what we are both talking about in terms of Sharpe's residence time. The challenge is to think about this indeterminacy: to unpack the different temporalities embedded in the space of the water, and the bodies within this space.

HG Perry's work is a great example of the experience of a loss of horizon. Through the immersive artwork that you just described, we can no longer separate our own viewpoint or space from the liquid world that surrounds us. And here it might be interesting to draw attention to the original definition of the term "immersion," which is the act or experience of being plunged or submerged in liquid. While we are drawn to the lower-right corner of Turner's image, where we can see a leg still in shackles, in Perry's digital reproduction of the image, the ocean is transformed and animated, and we don't see the body parts—but we know they are there.

Thus, Perry's immersive video installation turns to abstraction: it refers to early forms of violent abstraction in the context of slavery—from human being to market value—and hence to the early abstraction of modern financial capital that took place on the slave ship. (And here it is noticeable that abstraction also operates at the level of the work's title: Perry used only the final part of the title of Turner's painting to name her own work—the typhoon, a fiction imagined onto history, as you highlight in your essay.) But Perry's work also speaks to the radical potential of (audio)visual abstraction in the arts by turning away from a figurative, indexical representation of history—a strategy and politics of Black radical thought that we can also see in Saidiya Hartman's writing,[9] for example, as well as in Sharpe's.

You can see a similar turn away from the figurative form of representation in current discussions in queer theory, for example, particularly within trans studies/art/activism. In a recent discussion of "queer and trans* anarchitectural" performance art, Jack Halberstam focuses on what is not visible—similar to Perry's work, it seems—on "what has been destroyed, erased, or blacked out in order for what remains present to look permanent."[10]

One of the effects of this form of abstraction that suggests an oceanic embodiment, it seems, is a temporal disorientation in which complex processes of being/becoming are made tangible—for Halberstam, for example, it is less about a definite transition (from female to male, for example) than a constant "dismantling and remaking, a sculpting of flesh and molecular form."

We also looked together at Kitso Lynn Lelliott's video work *My story no doubt is me / Older than me* (2015). This video is part of a larger body of works in which she asks what it means to conceive of oneself as a giver of shape to ghosts. Interestingly, in this piece the camera is fixed on the horizon, and it's this emphasis on the horizon set against a backyard in Accra that produces a different sense of the real, as I argue in my text, as ghostly, ephemeral bodies appear and disappear, and the sky becomes alive. It would be great to hear your thoughts on this as I know this work resonates with your interest in bodies and stars.

AH One thing that strikes me about this film is this way in which Lelliott uses the sky, or what is above the horizon, to test out what is happening on earth. This ties in with the idea of vertical time that I explore in "Sea Changes": there is a temporal index in moving from above to below, whether the vertical movement is from the sky to the earth or from the surface of the water to its depths. This relates to the concept of revolutionary time that I mentioned earlier, the crisscrossing of the Atlantic by two different times and in two opposite directions. One of the things that I talk about is how revolutionary time could combine with vertical time to produce what I call transversal time.

To go back to the body, I want to end with an anecdote. I teach a class called "From Sky and Stars," for which one of my students, Arivan Shanmugaratnam, did a presentation on *Kindred*. In his presentation he mentioned the invocation of stars in this novel. There's one point in the novel when Dana escapes from the house that belongs to Rufus's father by night, and she gets knocked out. When she comes to, she looks up and she sees that the sky is starless. He also described a conversation that he had watched between Saidiya Hartman and Fred Moten, where Hartman described how, after certain passages across the Atlantic, when the slave ship arrived at its destination, the women sometimes came out of the ship with the shapes of stars and constellations carved into their hair. This is a celestial marking out of the journey that they went on. In these registers of body and territory drawing outward from the body lies transversal time.

1 Henriette Gunkel, Ayesha Hameed, and Simon O'Sullivan, eds., *Futures and Fictions* (London: Repeater Books, 2017).

2 Ayesha Hameed, "Black Atlantis," in *We Travel the Space Ways: Black Imagination, Fragments, and Diffractions*, ed. Henriette Gunkel and kara lynch (Bielefeld: transcript, 2019), 110.

3 See, for example, Hito Steyerl, "In Free Fall: A Thought Experiment on Vertical Perspective," *e-flux journal*, no. 24 (April 2011); and Laboria Cuboniks, *Xenofeminism: A Politics for Alienation*, 2015, http://laboriacuboniks.net.

4 Octavia E. Butler, Damien Duffy, and John Jennings, *A Graphic Novel Adaptation by Damien Duffy and John Jennings of Octavia E. Butler's "Kindred"* (New York: Abrams Books, 2018).

5 See Roland Barthes, *Camera Lucida* (New York: Hill & Wang, 1980); and Ariella Azoulay, *The Civil Contract of Photography* (New York: Zone Books, 2008).

6 Andrey Tarkovsky, *Sculpting in Time* (Austin: University of Texas Press, 1989).

7 Mark Fisher, "The Metaphysics of Crackle: Afrofuturism and Hauntology," *Dancecult: Journal of Electronic Dance Music Culture* 5, no. 2 (2013): 51.

8 Anna Coatman, "Sondra Perry on Blackness, Gender and Internet Culture," Royal Academy of Arts, March 6, 2018, https://www.royalacademy.org.uk/article/magazine-sondra-perry-typhoon-coming-on-serpentine-galleries.

9 See, for instance, Saidiya Hartman, *Scenes of Subjection: Terror, Slavery, and Self-Making in Nineteenth-Century America* (Oxford: Oxford University Press, 1997); and Hartman, *Lose Your Mother: A Journey along the Atlantic Slave Route* (New York: Farrar, Straus and Giroux, 2007).

10 Jack Halberstam, "Unbuilding Gender: Trans* Anarchitectures in and beyond the Work of Gordon Matta-Clark," *Places*, October 2018, https://placesjournal.org/article/unbuilding-gender/. The following quotation is also from this source.

SEA CHANGES AND OTHER FUTURISMS

AYESHA HAMEED

Speed

This is my first evening at Walkers, once a sugar plantation and now a dairy. It is dusk.

I step outside the house, climb the slightly mossy stairs, and turn right into the purpling light. To my left are horse stables, behind me is the house, and in front of me are fields of grass.

The sound of the frogs begins at dusk, and it gets louder. The paved drive I am walking on ends at the field, and I turn right onto a dirt path. The grass is long on either side of the path. When I reach a lone tree to my left, the path dips down a small hill and continues to a line of trees in the distance. To the right is the South, and there are some twinkling lights in the distance. A small bat swoops over my head.

Under the alien and screechy whirring of the frogs, there is a silence. A black dog runs up to me from the big house and then turns around and goes back, looking back at me as if trying to get me to follow it. I walk away from the dog and into the long grass, and listen.

The frogs get louder. The sky turns black.

*

Another beginning: It is half past two, and I've been waiting in the parking lot outside Harrison's Cave for about thirty minutes. Tour buses and hired taxis efficiently pull in and out of the parking spaces, loading and unloading their American passengers.

Two men are chatting beside me, one of them offers the other a lift, and they walk over to a brightly painted bus. I figure I have twenty minutes more to wait.

I hear a loud noise and look up from my book to see a diesel-powered minibus hurtling through the lot like a getaway car after a heist. It stops abruptly at a hasty angle near the bus stop where I'm sitting. The sign on the bus just says: "City." People climb out quickly, the engine rumbling.

As I climb the stairs of the bus, it speeds up again so fast that I trip into a seat. I pull myself up, holding out my two Barbadian dollars to the driver with an apologetic "Excuse me?" and the man in the passenger seat waves at me impatiently to sit down.

I look out the window as the bus hurtles down dirt roads hewn through fields of cane speckled with sun and dust. We screech to another stop, and the engine grumbles and roars.

Outside are the fields of cane and men and women waiting on the side of the road.

*

What is the relationship between climate change and plantation economies? This essay is an exploration of many things: the beginnings of a fourth chapter of an ongoing performance called *Black Atlantis*; visiting the heartland of one of the three stops of the triangular trade connecting West Africa, the Caribbean, and Northern Europe; and taking seriously Donna Haraway's and Anna Tsing's use of the term "Plantationocene," which connects the development of a plantation form of agricultural production to the beginning of our current geologic era.

The Plantationocene is a placeholder for the relationship between agriculture and the violent replacement of diverse farming tactics, forests, and pastures by monocropping. Its roots lie in the factorylike extractive structure of eighteenth-century plantations—the large-scale cultivation of single crops like sugar and cotton for export, carried out by enslaved and indentured laboring bodies forcibly transported across vast distances. Plantations eradicate the diversity of what is cultivated, devastating the land, violently exploiting and expropriating the bodies working on the land, and destroying any possible autonomy for self-sustenance for those living in these areas.

The notion of the Plantationocene suggests that the geologic force of humans on the planet's ecosystem is rooted in plantation slavery, with its instrumentalization of the soil for a singular kind of production and its violent enslavement of bodies to be used as machines to cultivate and harvest—and ideally to reproduce and sustain itself. As Tsing says, the Plantationocene is formed of "machines of replication," or "simplified ecologies, such as plantations, in which lifeworlds are remade as future assets."[1] In other words, it highlights the aftermath of a radical and violent incursion and its effects on lifeworlds that intertwine the human and the natural.

It is a nearly impossible endeavor to read an over-three-hundred-year history of plantations and their continually evolving social relations in the wake of the oldest instance of plantation slavery and in the continued presence of descendants of slaves and plantation owners and overseers, against the slow temporal swings that mark climate change. Reading a still living and present history against a slowly unraveling future of increasing frequencies of natural disasters, the warming of the ocean, the jeopardization of marine life, is incommensurable and probably pointless, as they operate on such different registers, and the possibility of finding common ground at ground level is almost nil.

*

*

Time Series / Horizontal Time

Flight canceled. After taking a bus across Denmark from Billund, the home of Lego toys, to Copenhagen, I stumble first onto a flight to Stockholm and then, at my wits' end and near tears, into a hotel in the airport at 2:00 a.m. Three hours later, I wake up and catch another tiny plane to Turku, flying low across the Baltic Sea and the ring of islands radiating and radiating inward. From coast to coast, there are islands scattered in the sea.

As my plane has arrived late, I will miss the ferry, so Taru has miraculously conjured up another ride for me to the island. I am to take a taxi to a gas station and there meet Outi (whom I have never met before), who will drive me to Seili. (She has a shock of red hair and two dogs that sit quietly in the back of the car. To my horror, she passes their leashes to me at a pit stop. But they are as gentle as lambs.)

Seili is an island a few hours' ferry ride from Turku, home to a marine research center for the University of Turku. We are staying and working on the site of a former mental hospital, the island's previous incarnation. I sleep, to my surprise, in a former cell, but my window opens up on to a tree, and I see the sky still bright at night with midsummer sun.

The next day, as we are all standing in the courtyard waiting for a tour of the research labs and the former asylum, Outi appears quietly beside me and says, "Come with me." This is not a request. We walk away from the group to a building across the courtyard. Outi tells me she has been thinking about the story I told her the day before behind *Black Atlantis*, of Drexciyans jettisoned off slave ships adapting to life underwater and forming submarine cities.[2] I had told the group about how Drexciyans, the aquatic descendants of slaves thrown overboard from slave ships, evolved to develop gills to breathe underwater and later flippers for wave jumping. As we are walking into the building, Outi tells me that what I should have said is that Drexciyans became *acclimatized* to living underwater; this was different to adapting. I wondered what she meant.

She takes me to a room full of tanks off the main corridor. Each tank is filled with water, and tethered to the bottom of each boxy seafloor, bobbing in the bubbles, are bits of seaweed. The light is greenish and eerie; the room is quiet except for the sound of the water pumps. There is a woman pulling out a sample from one of the tanks. Outi tells me that my story made her think about these seaweed studies they were doing at the institute. We continue into a second room with a similar array of tanks.

Outi explains to me that what I am looking at is a time series. Each tank, meticulously labeled, has a different level of salinity. One of the effects of climate change in the Baltic Sea is rising salt levels. In order to predict what levels of salt the seaweed can survive in, samples from the same plant are put into tanks, each with a different amount of salt. Each tank, then, is a model of a possible future state of the sea. And this capacity for seaweed, low on the food chain, to acclimatize to increasing levels of salinity becomes a measure of the threshold of whether life can be sustained.

What I was looking at was a predictive model. Each tank represented a slice of time from the future. But it is time laid out in space, side by side. Time becomes a spatial, sequential model staged all together in a continuous present. This is a time series.

Laying out time as sequence, spatially arranged, is echoed in another maritime account of climate violence: in a 2017 presentation for the Kochi-Muziris Biennale in India, Dilip Menon describes the use of floods, cyclones, and submersions in the Indian Ocean to speak of the quality of maritime and aquatic insurgencies. He turns to Marie Velardi's *Atlas des îles perdues 2107*, a series of drawings arranged in a line and set in what he calls a "time that is to come":

> Sketches of islands that exist, islands that have ceased to exist, and islands that *will* cease to exist. And by 2107, all of these islands will be under the ocean. So when you walk into this room, what you are seeing before you is the past, present and future on this wall. Where the world has been flooded; the world is flooding, and the flood waters are rising. [...] So the *Atlas des îles perdues 2107* talks about a passage of time within a static frame: the islands that exist, the islands that will vanish, the islands that have already vanished.[3]

Menon describes the sequence of the drawings of islands in spatiotemporal terms similar to those of the time series. Differences in time are presented on a single horizontal plane in images arranged across the wall. Each island

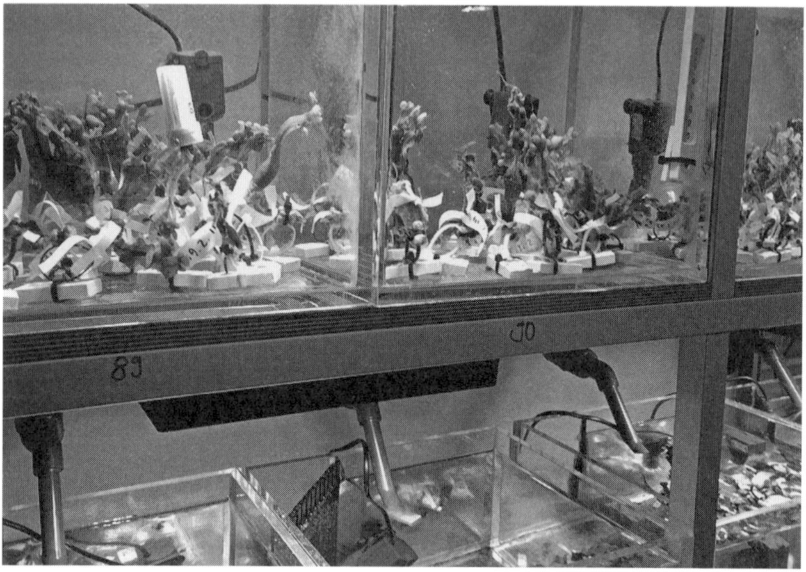

TIME SERIES WITH SAMPLES FROM THE BALTIC SEA, ARCHIPELAGO RESEARCH INSTITUTE, SEILI FIELD STATION, 2017

evokes the slice of time of its own extinction. What brings the sequence of images onto a single spatial plane is the horizontal axis where they meet across time—that is, at their different moments of annihilation. The time of their submersion is spatialized across the wall. This time series of islands is scaled up in size from the seaweed in the tanks at Seili, but the index of the scale of the disaster is the same. It is a measure of the threshold of survivability, or the limit of acclimatization. And all these temporalities are presented in a single moment that is experienced by the viewer looking at the time-series sequence. With time jumping from image to image and yet also coalesced into the same moment, what is the temporality of the viewer and what affordances do we have as we look at this sequence of images or the tanks filled with seaweed? When are we?

Something happens to time when it is sequenced spatially, but something happens to space as well. There are two spaces: the space of the sequence and the space to which the timescale refers, which in this instance is the ocean and the sea over time and into the future. This is the imbricated time-space of the maritime, and also island time.

This is the experiment: What if a time series formed the basis for thinking time travel? But time, that is, impregnated with island maritime space on the precipice of destruction. This proposition is drawn from Antonio Benítez-Rojo's *The Repeating Island*, where he sees the Antilles as an archipelago that can only be comprehended through the repetitions afforded by its chaotic structure and bridgelike connection to the Americas: "This geographical accident gives the entire area, including its continental foci, the character of an archipelago, that is, a discontinuous conjunction (of what?): unstable condensations, turbulences, whirlpools, clumps of bubbles, frayed seaweed, sunken galleons, crashing breakers, flying fish, seagull squawks, downpours, nighttime phosphorescences, eddies and pools, uncertain voyages of signification; in short, a field of observation quite in tune with the objectives of Chaos."[4] In other words, "Chaos" is built into the geologic and maritime qualities of the Antilles, and within this kinetic and dynamic set of factors there are patterns, regularities, repetitions, which according to Benítez-Rojo converge as a repeating island that cannot be materialized.

The reverberations of the repeating island move centrifugally to connect to other seas around the world:

> Within the sociocultural fluidity that the Caribbean archipelago presents, within its historiographic turbulence and its ethnological and linguistic clamor, within its generalized instability of vertigo and hurricane, one can sense the features of an island that "repeats" itself, unfolding and bifurcating until it reaches all the seas and lands of the earth. [...] The Caribbean is not a common archipelago, but a meta-archipelago [...], and as a meta-archipelago it has the virtue of having neither a boundary nor a center. Thus the Caribbean flows outward past the limits of its own sea with a vengeance, and its *ultima Thule* may be found on the outskirts of Bombay, near the low and murmuring shores of Gambia, in

> a Cantonese tavern of circa 1850, at a Balinese temple, in an old Bristol pub, in a commercial warehouse in Bordeaux at the time of Colbert, in a windmill beside the Zuider Zee, at a cafe in a barrio of Manhattan, in the existential *saudade* of an old Portuguese lyric. But what is it that repeats? Tropisms, in series; movements in approximate direction.[5]

What Benítez-Rojo means is that, by dint of its centrality to the history of slavery and the development of the Industrial Revolution, the meta-archipelago of the Antilles exerts a centrifugal force of tropes and movements to other seas and shores. This repetition of "tropes" comes into being through the eddying currents and turbulences of natural forces.

The island repeats through what, evoking Gilles Deleuze and Félix Guattari, he calls the Caribbean machine—connecting mines to flotillas and ports, and characterized by flows and interruptions in the movement between one and the other. These starts and stops, interruptions and flows, temporal fuel for the machine, would stutter to a halt without the most central machine of all: the plantation. It is the force of the plantation that jettisons the centrifugal force of the repeating island to every sea and shore. It is the fundamental machine of capitalism.

The repeating island of the Plantationocene is, then, the swirls and the eddies and the ferment of cyclones and the ontology of the water, the Chaos, coupled with the repetition, the flows, the interruptions, and the inexorable chain of chains of the machines at whose heart lies the machine of the plantation:

> We should think of [mines] as machines joined to other machines; we should see them in terms of production (flow and interruption). Such mining machines, by themselves, would not have been much help in accumulating European capital. Without the Caribbean machine (from Columbus's prototype to the working model of Menéndez de Avilés), Europeans would have been in the absurd position of the gambler who hits the jackpot at the slot machine but who has no hat in which to catch his winnings.[6]

What Benítez-Rojo evokes is a kind of phantasmagoria of time, following Walter Benjamin's description through the medium of gambling, which turned "time into a narcotic" to be endlessly traded for itself.[7] In this instance, however, the phantasmagoria endlessly trades space for time. The gambler is caught up in the narcotic of time and, in this haze, re-creates a series of gestures that recapitulate the industrial machine. But here the machine is the Caribbean.[8]

Outi and I return to the group, who are walking away from a map of the Baltic Sea that covers the length and height of an entire wall of the lab that was once an asylum. "What did I miss?" I ask Joshua. He pulls out his phone and shows me a map of the Baltic Sea. "This," he says. I see a circle of islands arranged around a center that is not an island, but the sea. "What is it?" I ask. Islands arranged centrifugally away from a meteor that crashed into the empty middle that is only sea. There is a force moving outward from that empty middle, a kind of eddying arrangement of forces and land whose contiguity and radiation somehow confuses me. I take a picture of Joshua's screen and his hand holding the phone. In the center is the silence of the water.

And this machine of the plantation, fueled by the temporal qualities of alternation and interruption—the flux and chaos of nature in revolt—when coupled with the time series, its spatialization of time in a sequence, its creation of an indeterminate present for the spectator of the time series, becomes the means with which to time travel, to build a time machine.

The logic that pulls the Baltic Sea time series into contiguity with the Antillean repeating island, as a way to understand time travel in the Plantationocene, is the intuitive first step. More specifically, drawing a link between these two disparate spaces enhances the interrupting and flowing temporality of the plantation machine, with the temporal expansion into the deep geologic and historical time of the Plantationocene, and the code-switching of the future, into the space of the time series.

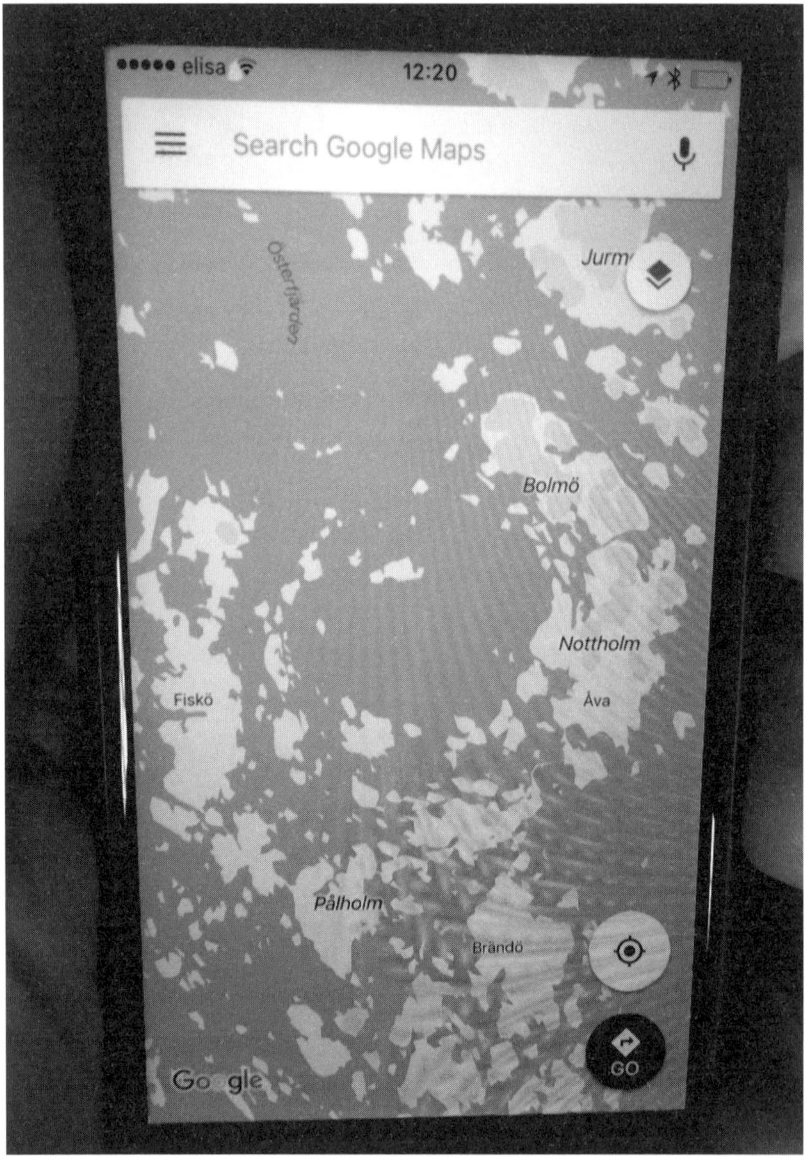

CIRCLE OF ISLANDS IN THE BALTIC SEA VIEWED ON A MOBILE VERSION OF GOOGLE MAPS, 2017

All of this is inextricable from maritime and island time. As Elizabeth DeLoughrey describes in her literary study of Maori temporality, with the intensification of climate change, sea levels are rising, and consequently more and more of the earth is maritime. For Marie Velardi, islands are sinking and turning into the sea. And for DeLoughrey, "our planetary future is becoming more oceanic."[9] The sea is temporalized as the future, and our experience of the future can only be oceanic. The resources in the ocean are also the site of bioprospecting and venture capitalism.[10] The future is oceanic, and the futures market is also blue.

DeLoughrey describes what she calls an adaptive geontology that takes from this temporalization of the ocean in order to understand the imbricatedness of humans in maritime spaces. From this perspective, climate change is inseparable from the boundaries of human action, thrown into relief when scaled down to the quotidian and the everyday. She draws this reading of the ordinary maritime quality of climate violence from a Maori worldview, connected to deep geologic time: "This turn to nonapocalyptic models of climate change requires different models of temporality. [...] In the Maori language one puts the past in front while one moves backward into the future [...]. This narrative merger with fossils (and later the sea) suggests an encounter with deep planetary time that renders an interspecies relationship."[11] From the Maori perspective, the past lies in front and the future lies behind. In other words, this worldview reverses a Western temporality that looks forward into the future. It is a perspective intertwined with nature, geologic time, and the sea. And this (from a Western point of view) reversed spatialization of time is complemented by an image in Polynesian cosmology: "Ala Moana, the way of the ocean, refers in many Polynesian cultures to the past in which Indigenous voyagers settled across the expanse of the Pacific as well as to the future, in which one's departing spirit joins the 'ocean roads' toward Hawaiki (or Hawai'i), a homeland located outside of terrestrial models of space and time."[12] The past moves forward, and the future moves backward. A journey across the ocean is at once into the future and outside of space and time. The Polynesian journey across the ocean and away from terrestrial time, combined with the reversal of time in the Maori perspective, signals the immanent possibility of the unmooring of time. Together, they blur the registers of the human into oceanic temporalities.

Consider this unmooring in conjunction with the already heightened temporal interruption and flow of the Plantationocene machine and the indeterminate present/presence of one witnessing the spatiotemporal leaps of the time series. The Plantationocene, when temporally fueled, leads to this time machine. The order of the time sequence is scrambled by the viewer, who moves forward in space and yet backward in time. The Plantationocene veers from deep geologic history to unthinkable climate futures, but these registers are scaled down, reversed into one another, and their boundaries made more porous. This is a beginning of time travel in medias res.

*

*

Fire

Annalee tells me she loves the smell of sugar. Once when she was young, there was a fire in one of the fields on the plantation. Her father, who was hired to oversee the farm, went out into the fields. One of the workers was driving a new tractor that caught fire. Her father was reluctant to lose the truck, and so climbed into the driver's seat to extinguish the flames. He came home that night, she said, with the skin of his arm bubbling and burned.

Often at night fires were deliberately set in the fields in order to damage the crops. There is an entire history as to why. On those nights, the air was filled with the smell of burning sugar. It was sweet.

In Barbados, cane fields are not set on fire like the sugar fields I had seen in Colombia, where the cane cutters get covered in black soot from head to toe as they swing their machetes into cane stalks several meters high. Standing at the edge of the field then, I had watched the flakes of soot come floating down like snow while being bitten by insects so small I could not see them, and so hard that I still have scars from when the bites got infected.

Here in Barbados, there is no need to clear the ground of vermin for the incoming cutters. There are no dangerous vermin, and the cutters are machines now. Unburned cane is more valuable anyway.

*

Nicolai tells me about Trinidad Carnival. A few of us had decided to go for a drink at the bar across the street. It was pouring rain, and as we sprinted into the bar the sound of the rain was muted by the loud music, which we had to shout over. After a few *what?!*s, we jumped into the car and drove to the mall down the street. We walked through a series of courtyards where, in the open air, a band was playing parang music. The rain was still falling and the band was alone under the sky, the audience clustered in around the building. We walk into a bar nearby.

The wall is lined with TV screens, each showing a movie trailer or a sports telecast. Nicolai tells me about J'ouvert. J'ouvert—a combination of *jour* and *ouvert*—is the first Carnival event, a procession that winds through the city at night into daybreak. J'ouvert is populated by devils, he tells me: a red devil, a blue devil, a devil devil named Jab Jab (from "Diable, diable!"), and a molasses devil named Jab Molassie. On the night of J'ouvert, I am told, you cover yourself in red paint or blue paint to align yourself with the red or blue devils. Those following Jab Molassie cover themselves in molasses or petroleum. Why petroleum *or* molasses? I ask. Because they are staples, Nicolai says. Trinidad has its own supply of natural gas and oil. Others cover themselves in chocolate, from another staple, cocoa.

Force. I go home and look up Jab Molassie on the internet. Legend has it that Jab Molassie came into being when a slave was thrown into a vat of molasses and returned as a devil. His skin is covered in black molasses. On this night of Carnival, Jab Molassie can also be covered in oil. Why isn't he then called Jab Pétrole? Petroleum is somehow an equal signifier in the darkness of the night of J'ouvert. The monocrop is the murderer as well as the avenging force of the murdered. Blackness covers the night. The sugar and petroleum wreak their revenge in the body of Jab Molassie. Or the force of resistance is in the viscous medium of molasses and oil.

All of this starts with fire. When fire broke out on a sugarcane plantation, overseers would force slaves into the burning fields and harvest the cane in the smoke and fire, to save what was salvageable. They worked to the beat of shells and horns, and the flick of whips.

J'ouvert possibly originated in an event called Canboulay, or Cannes Brulées (French for "burnt cane"). Canboulay was a procession of plantation owners and overseers who parodied this forced harvest of cane by fire by dressing as enslaved men and women (*nègres de jardin*) marching through the streets with flaming torches.

After 1834 came the era of the Jamette Carnival, or carnival of the dispossessed, where emancipated men and women parodied the parodies of their former owners, walking the streets with torches made of burning sugarcane stalks, beating drums and blowing horns. They were accompanied by stick fighters who had their own music. Some even dressed in the costume of the *nègres de jardin*, some wearing rags and others wielding whips. During this period, fights broke out among the revelers along fault lines of race, religion, ethnicity, and language, as indentured laborers from India joined the ranks of workers and, consequently, the streets.

The first objects to be outlawed in Carnival are the torches, the drums, and the sticks, in 1868. But they stay for another dozen years until the burning torches and burning sugar fields of Canboulay are purged from Carnival.

*

We climb in through the window of the empty building. Scattered in the room are ledgers, shards of broken glass, and old journals. There are beaker stands and bottles of what look like toxic chemicals on the dusty shelves. Further inside, the room gets darker and darker.

It is dusk, nearing six o'clock. I look through an opening to my left and see a large room, sunk two stories deep and already in shadows. The stringy sound of the frogs' chorus emanates from that empty room into this smaller one.

The air is sickly sweet as if its memory of the sugar is still fresh. I walk through the doorway into a suspended corridor and the smell gets stronger. There are large vats and measures and equipment at the end of the corridor whose purpose I can intuit. Everything is rusty and broken.

I test a flight of stairs and climb up slowly to another suspended corridor, one eye on the termite's nest at the bottom of the stairs. But the airy promise of height and possible perspective is too enticing to ignore. I am hoping to see something more in this old, disused, and still sticky, sweet-smelling building, and maybe the height will help.

Beams of light cut high up the wall through the dust.

The roof is stories above me, and I see a single cable suspended from it. At the end of the cable, at eye level, hangs a large round lightbulb still intact.

*

*

Atlantis

After day after day after day of sun in the morning, sun in the afternoon, rain sliced through the sky in a gash. The rainy season has just ended, but at its margins there is still the threat of water. This has taken center stage, today of all days. The taxi drives up to the house, and the rain is so fat and plummy that it is impossible to sprint up the stairs to the car door without getting wet.

The taxi approaches the outskirts of the city with the wipers barely clearing the view. Each stroke of the blade makes a grating sound. We drive past the terminal where all the ocean liners anchor, their bulky bodies indistinct in the distance with the thickness of the pelting water. And then we arrive at the Atlantis office. It is brightly colored and full of tourist memorabilia: rum and beaches in the shape of coasters and keychains. There is some free fruit punch in the corner. On the wall is a mural, a window painted and encrusted to look like coral. There are two TVs on either side of the room—one with a documentary promo about our destination on loop, the other tuned to CNN with its endless loop of Trump winning the Electoral College vote in late December.

We wait.

Two overwhelmed parents try to keep their identically dressed daughters calm on what appears to be their birthday. Busloads of tourists arrive, and they watch these two children indulgently, or look at CNN. We all sit on purple leather benches. Outside the rain lashes at the windows.

Finally, the door opens, and we are ushered out to walk the hundred meters to the waiting boat. It is raining so hard that we are instructed to share the umbrellas they hand us. Still, I am drenched by the time I get to the boat. After a safety demonstration, and lots of loud music, we head off. The water is gray and the sky is also gray. The rain falls so thickly on the window that the seascape falls into blurry pixels. Finally, we reach a point in the middle of the water where a small metal structure protrudes from underwater. We've arrived at the Atlantis submarine.

*

In the early twentieth century, John Ernest Williamson, son of an English sea captain, was energized by stories about lost Atlantises and the sinking of pirate towns like Port Royal in Jamaica. With his brother George, he designed and built a structure called the "photosphere," an underwater chamber with a glass panel that was connected to a boat on the surface of the water by a tube made of concentric rings.

Williamson moved to the Bahamas to build his photosphere because the surrounding waters are shallow and the coral sand is sparkling and white. The sea is largely free of clouding phytoplankton, so the water is clear. The photosphere was used for a number of purposes: as a chamber from which to film the first underwater moving images; as a tourist novelty, where visitors could send postcards from the bottom of the sea through an underwater post office; and, reportedly, for underwater salvage. It is here that the 1916 film *20,000 Leagues under the Sea* was filmed, the figures ghostly still.

Krista A. Thompson, in her study of the Caribbean picturesque, describes how dreamlike these early immersions into the photosphere were, but adds that the underwater vista was also perceived to be menacing. This was reflected in Williamson's own thinking and in his lecture "Beauty and Tragedy under the Sea," which he delivered to audiences in Great Britain, Ireland, and the United States. Not only was Bahamian land remarkably fertile, but its marine life was blooming and multiplying.

In the late nineteenth century, a fascination with underwater life as a kind of spectacle flourished as an elite pastime. Young Black men would dive to the bottom of the sea to grab mementos for genteel women waiting on boats who peered into the sea through "tropical lorgnons"—glass-bottomed buckets. The submarine world was seen as an underwater garden, a landscape or a forest. The traveler William Hutchinson, for example, "re-envisioned coral sponges as 'welcoming palms,' fish as 'hummingbirds,' and coral as 'great trees' and 'stately forests' [...]. Charles Ives also contended that the seascape bore similarity to 'the vast and magnificent tropical forests, clothed in perennial green, adorned with graceful vines, teeming with flowers of every hue, and vocal with countless birds of the most varied and of the richest plumage, bear to a lady's little but luxurious boudoir, with its evergreen branches, climbing vines and captive birds in their small but gilded cages.'"[13]

*

The geographer Jessica Lehman's study of the archival properties of the ocean describes the sinking of the Dutch slave ship *Leusden* in Atlantic waters off the coast of Suriname in 1738. The captain nailed shut the hatches to the hold of the ship, which held 680 women, men, and children. Although well-documented, the wreck has never been found. Thinking of the ocean depths as an archive, she writes: "If the ocean has concealed some of slavery's ruins, it has not so readily hidden all of the more recent traces of capitalist imperialism. In July 1964, during one episode in a long history of marine toxic dumping, the British merchant vessel *Halcience* began to discard packages of radioactive waste from several state-operated sites into the Bay of Biscay."[14] Lehman connects the modern history of toxic dumping to the sinking of slave ships, the ocean a repository and archive defined by ruin. While radioactive waste arguably has left more traces on the surface, the residues of the slave ships lie in the Atlantic's undersea currents, which she argues, following Édouard Glissant, are "signposted by 'scarcely corroded' balls and chains."[15]

And then there are the corroded currents themselves, waves laced with oil after the *Deepwater Horizon* oil spill in 2010, where 210 gallons of oil and natural gas slicked down the continental slope into deep water. This Atlantis is not an *archive* of the dead, the radioactive, the oil-slicked, and the corroded. It *is* all these things. This is its tragedy.

*

*

Vertical Time / Transversal Time

Item

In July 2017, the *New York Times* reported a story about George Church and Seth Shipman, geneticists and researchers at Harvard Medical School, who encoded frames from Eadweard Muybridge's 1878 photographic sequence of a galloping horse into the DNA of a living cell. This encoding was performed using CRISPR, a gene-editing software, which assigned a shade of gray to each of the four molecules composing all configurations of DNA, based on the pixel they represented in Muybridge's image.

The moving image of the galloping horse was found to maintain its integrity over several generations of bacteria. At a molecular level, then, this is an encoding of time in a movie that operates as a witness, a producer of testimony that is made of the same material it bears witness to. The science-fiction fantasy of this encoding goes further: it projects a future where bacterial DNA could record the activity of the cells they are attached to. One day, bacteria could act as a black box recording the illnesses and cellular life of the bodies they live in. Time, witnessing, and bacteria become intertwined and, as a result, detached from their referents at a molecular level. Together, they tell another set of stories.

Item

Dust report. The oldest records of dust transport date from 1965 in Ragged Point, Barbados. Trade winds blowing across the Atlantic, from the Sahel to the Caribbean and beyond, make up about 70 percent of the global distribution of dust. It takes a week for dust to cross the ocean and disintegrate in the friction of its flight. These grains of dust are rich in iron and phosphorous. Dust travels across the Atlantic, spreading iron into the ocean's carbon cycle and providing marine microorganisms with a vital micronutrient.[16] This dust also forms deposits in the soil in the Bahamas and Caribbean—adding phosphorous and other nutrients to the soil all the way into the Amazon basin, and much-needed iron deposits in the Atlantic Ocean.[17] Before merging with land or sea, airborne dust has an impact on the weather and climate of the Caribbean. It can affect the growth of cyclones and the temperature of sea surfaces, which in turn could affect hurricane activity and cloud microphysics.[18] Dust is also linked to health issues. Throughout the Caribbean, there is widespread asthma, which might be connected to the prevalence of dust. Half of the dust that crosses from the Sahel is less than 2.5 µm in diameter, which is categorized by United States Environmental Protection Agency standards as "respirable" or inhalable. In epidemiological studies, respirable dust has been correlated with asthma, chronic bronchitis, and other severe respiratory symptoms.[19]

Dust moves both horizontally across the ocean and land and vertically into the depths of the earth, the sea, and into human bodies and lungs. Regarding the latter, one cannot help but recall the words of Bataille: "The storytellers have not realized that the Sleeping Beauty would have awoken covered in a thick layer of dust; nor have they envisaged the sinister spiders' webs that would have been torn apart at the first movement of her red tresses. Meanwhile dismal sheets of dust constantly invade earthly habitations and uniformly defile them: as if it were a matter of making ready attics and old rooms for the imminent occupation of the obsessions, phantoms, spectres that the decayed odour of old dust nourishes and intoxicates."[20]

*

Question. What is the time of dust and of cellular matter?

Answer.
Here are intimations that the machine of the Plantationocene not only moves horizontally across land and sea but also plummets into the depths of body tissue and molecular life. What role does the CRISPR cells' movie play in the machine of the Plantationocene? This can be at first understood by returning to Benítez-Rojo: "In truth, the field in which Chaos may be observed is extremely vast, for it includes all phenomena that depend on the passage of time; Chaos looks toward everything that repeats, reproduces, grows, decays, unfolds, flows, spins, vibrates, seethes; it is as interested in the evolution of the solar system as in the stock market's crashes, as involved in cardiac arrhythmia as in the novel or in myth."[21] Benítez-Rojo's description of Chaos as operating on the register of both the body and

the solar system, that is, as both scalar and embodied, comes close to the multiplication of time that the machine of the Plantationocene—with its own enslaved bodies—needs to take into account. In the first instance, this scalar time has the quality of verticality; it probes both the depths of tissue matter and territory.

To move deeper into tissue is to move in time. This is a relationship with the sediment. Dust writ large is a temporal symptom of the passage of time and of accumulating sedimentary layers. Dust in its microcosmic form is what we breathe in or what makes breath difficult.

Kathryn Yusoff's notion of "geologic time" implicates this temporal conjunction of body and territory that highlights its verticality. Geologic time recognizes that our origins are interconnected with geologic sedimentations, and that as a species we humans will end up as a set of sedimented fossils as well. The shock of this confrontation of origins and ends produces the spectral beginnings of time travel. In imagining ourselves as fossils, humans become "an object that has collided with its spectre to provide its own haunting."[22]

In other words, this horizon of ends produces a kind of collision of self with the specter of a future self, but this also plays out in the temporal awareness of the sedimentation of geologic strata. There is, consequently, a futurity built into the geologic strata, Yusoff argues, and this plays out on the terrain of the archaeological, the verticality of the cross-section of the earth, moving vertically downward:

> To imagine ourselves a fossil is to become the body/thing that is abandoned to time and given over to the chaotic churnings of the earth. Implicit in this imagining is a model of the earth as strata: vertical rather than horizontal territory; intensified by the passage of time; in layers that press hard on the possibilities of forms that become fragmented in time and material integrity. The fossil then is an abandoned being that suddenly in the midst of the present reconfigures the possibilities of times, of past and future, and like a line of flight thrown from

> some prehistoric world it offers a hitherto unimaginable direction to thought and becoming. This is the temporal and spatial scene in which fossils speak.[23]

It is this verticality that reconfigures the fossil, bringing into its composition both past and future. The complicity between body and sediment, or body and the geologic/geographic, goes even further through the medium of bone. It cuts transversally into the body akin to the movie made up of bacterial sequences. "De Landa reminds us that the origins of our bodily composition are a form of mineralization that is always on the threshold between the biological vitality of bone and the dead matter of the fossil, and ready to cross back into the geologic record at a moment's notice."[24]

Scaled down. In their spatial study of police violence and urban planning in the United States, Lindsey Dillon and Julie Sze connect dust and the ability to breathe as an "important spatiality through which to critique contemporary relations of power."[25] Dillon and Sze reexamine Eric Garner's murder in a choke hold by the police. Garner, an asthma sufferer, repeated "I can't breathe" before dying. His last words became a key slogan in the Black Lives Matter movement, but they also resonate with environmental justice on a broader level: Dillon and Sze describe the prevalence of asthma sufferers in Black communities, and connect this to urban renewal, including highway construction, which increases exposure to air pollution. Consequently, there is a high correlation between race and incidences of asthma.

Asthma, like dust, is created by factors that are both external and internal to bodies, they argue, as are illnesses like hypertension, diabetes, and obesity. The authors argue that this is inextricable from racial segregation in the United States. Garner's death is an environmental and racial issue with a long history. Being able to breathe is a matter of racial privilege: "In this vein, we interpret the phrase 'I can't breathe' as condensing the histories of persistent patterns of pollution and police violence, both of which have denied breath and healthy breathing spaces to low-income communities of color. In this sense, the inability to breathe can be understood as both a metaphor and material reality of racism, which constrains not just life choices and opportunities, but the environmental conditions of life itself."[26] To deny breath is to deny the humanity of one trying to breathe. Scaled down, the particulate matter of dust infiltrates the body, and makes indissoluble the transition from dust to membrane. Scaled up, the dust of the highway and of urban renewal provides the topography for dusty lungs. Bones become fossils and back again, dust enters lungs, carpets, cities, becomes a weapon no less systemic than the choke hold laying Eric Garner to the ground.

Breathing in dust particles juxtaposes two temporalities: the future/anterior vectors of the fossil that is ingested, and the gasping body that is mired in the present and in crisis. This is an incursion of one time—of fossils (slow, future/anterior)—into another time, that of the body-at-this-moment (rapid, present). Materially, dust crosses the membrane dividing the body from its environment and becomes part of the body. Temporally, future and anterior time infiltrate the membrane of the present in crisis.

There is no air, only dust. When there is no breath, it is death.

*

Question. How to plot this in island time?

Answer.
Drexciyan bodies skew this equation by changing the substance of breath from air into water. They can breathe, but breathing is something else in an improbable time.

Water is made of strata that are sedimented and carry portents of other times, both anticipatory and remembered. This is material. Nicholas Mirzoeff, in his 2017 essay "Below the Water: Black Lives Matter and Revolutionary Time," follows the trajectory of cyclones across the Atlantic, and points out that the direction of the winds follows that of the slave ships several centuries ago.

> After Hurricane Katrina devastated New Orleans in 2005, there was much discussion about the fact that hurricanes seem to follow the same route taken by the slave ships. It was said that spirits from the Middle Passage (like the Haitian *lwa* Simbi) had destroyed the city in their anger over slavery. Why would the spirits destroy African-American homes over slavery, rather than those of slavers? They are nonhuman and think differently. They want to take their human counterparts "back to Africa." In Kreyol, that connection is called *anba dlo* (beneath the water).

This nauticalization of Black Lives Matter forms the creation of what he calls "revolutionary time below the water." Mirzoeff explains:

> Revolutionary time allows for the unexpunged potential of a moment to be reanimated. A dialectical image catches such potential and contains it, waiting for the moment in which it can again be seen for what it is. Revolutionary time has never left the place of possibility, rather than trying to contain it in norms and hierarchies. In revolutionary time, actors experience the future in real time because the intensity of their contact with others takes place so quickly that it is to experience in days what otherwise might take months or years. Revolutionary time is more like cosmological time than it is like capitalist time.[27]

For Mirzoeff, it is no strange coincidence that the routes of the slave ships are retraced by the indiscriminate destructive force of hurricanes and cyclones, as a kind of return of matter in waiting. It undoes the dictates of clock time in industrial modes of production under capitalism. Instead, it is the recapitulation of a time in the past that has reversed its force and direction of destruction, drawing from the violent movement of the slave ships it retraces and reappropriates. This primordial dialectical image captures in its force the bodies of descendants of the enslaved, taking them into the ocean, across the ocean, and below the ocean. This is the labor of *anba dlo*. Here, a gesture of translation is enacted in moving across the ocean; it is a spatiotemporal leap that reckons with the past while cycling the future into the present.

Fossils that connect bodies to their environments find their counterpart in the materialization of underwater space. Like geologic time, sedimentations in the sea can be read temporally and vertically. The mineralization of bodies in water is part of what Christina Sharpe calls "residence time": the persistence, at a molecular level, of enslaved bodies decomposing in water, solids turning to salinity as bones turn to calcium, and vice versa. This is the temporalization of organic matter becoming inorganic and flipping back again.

The threshold between ocean and body is not only eroded in the mineralization of bodies but also by rethinking the threshold of what constitutes living matter in the life of the ocean. DeLoughrey describes how the sea meets the liveliness of the human body in its mutability. This materializes the strata of water just as the erosion of bodies in residence time temporalizes them:

> The discourse of the Anthropocene positions humans as a geological force, yet the ocean seems to be our proxy. This raises questions as to the mutability between humans and the seas. While we recognize an anthropogenic climate, new science is suggesting a rather anthropomorphic ocean—perhaps even a super organism. Water's mutability, measured in picoseconds, means that it changes its molecular structure around one trillion times a second and has been likened to a network. Recent work on the ocean as superorganism has focused on the blurring between chemistry and living beings, as well as the "bacterial networking" [...] of the ocean's microbial communities.[28]

This blurring of what constitutes the threshold of life has a temporal register, the picosecond axis of molecular change in the sea. Returning to the molecular and to the measuring of units of time in order to map the constitution of a maritime space also returns us to a Drexciyan pivot: the possibility of human fetuses adapting from amniotic fluid to seawater, and therefore able to breathe underwater after being born.

As Outi and I were looking at the water tanks in Seili, she told me she was thinking about my remark about Drexciyans adapting to living underwater, and that I was wrong. Like the seaweed we were looking at, she thought that Drexciyans would have acclimatized to living in the sea. There was no change at the level of their DNA; rather, it was a stretching of the existing characteristics of these unborn children. At first I was puzzled, as developing gills and breathing underwater, and subsequently developing flippers, did seem like a more fundamental change. Later on, I remembered recapitulation theory: that ontogeny recapitulates phylogeny; that as it develops, the fetus represents each stage of evolution. What if the fetus just got off at an earlier stop on the evolutionary bus that it replicates in miniature in the womb? Recapitulation of an earlier stage of development to an improbable acclimatization to living underwater: moving simultaneously forward and backward in time. In other words, the mutability of the matter of bodies and of the matter of water are immanently time-traveling states. DeLoughrey again, with reference to Hawaiian and Maori understandings of temporality:

> Time is registered by a syntactic movement between present- and past-continuous tense by a narrator who, in the first line of the story, is "thinking back" to the omens before the launch, and then is interrupted by the present voice, an "I" who is "balanced on the end bollard" [...]. Thus dynamic earthly change is [...] being experienced in the interwoven tenses of an immediate present and past. This highlights the experience of climate change as a contemporaneous experience in the Pacific, as well as Maori epistemologies that position the past in front while the future is behind.[29]

This is vertical time, but plotted transversally. Narration is disrupted, time is mutable with the mutability of the water and the intermediate past and present blurring into one another.

*

*

<------------>

Coasts

I meet Aaron again after twelve years when he picks me up for a drive around the island. We decide to go to the Atlantic coast, the first of two trips. It seems like a set of journeys of attrition, as during the first trip we drive to a village called Bathsheba, and the second to another part of the coast called Bath. I'm convinced that had we made a third trip, it would have conjured a third stretch called Ba. But this kind of bad humor can't hold.

The Atlantic coast is the wild coast of the island. The water here is choppy, the settlements more sporadic, and the roads more intermittent and winding. As we drive down a sunny road, we see a woman waiting patiently by its side. Aaron stops and offers her a lift to work, which turns out to be a restaurant on the waterfront called the Roundhouse, which apparently serves great cocktails. "How were you planning to get there?" he asks her, and she points to a tiny path that disappears in the long grass. "Not a great idea," he says as we drive to the restaurant, and she agrees. "Next cocktail is on me," she calls as she climbs out of the car, and waves.

The first time I jump into the Atlantic, I feel the water pull and push against my skin. It is warm and swirling. The sand beneath my feet is rocky and rough. The beach is empty. Behind me in the sand are stumps of wood evenly placed, remnants of a railway track used to transport sugar along the coast. The coast has receded since then, and the stumps that once circled dry land are now half underwater.

I look to the east, across the water, and realize there is no land in sight. Following my gaze, Aaron tells me that the next landmass is the Senegalese coast. I keep staring east.

*

On April 29, 2006, a twenty-foot-long boat was spotted off Ragged Point, on the southeastern coast of Barbados. On board, eleven bodies were found by the coastguard, preserved and desiccated by the sun and saltwater. This was a ghost ship adrift for four months on the Atlantic Ocean. It set sail on Christmas Day from Praia in Cape Verde, full of migrants from Senegal, Guinea-Bissau, and the Gambia, en route to the Canary Islands. Each of these people paid £890 for their place on the boat.

The boat ran into trouble at Nouadhibou, a Mauritian port, and was towed for a time by another ship. An article in the *Guardian* conjectures that the line was possibly severed by a machete. Once adrift, this ship began its slow movement across the Atlantic, buffeted by the winds and rain, and pulled westward by the ocean's currents. By January, all the passengers had died, many of their bodies either jettisoned into the sea or washed overboard. This ghost ship then traveled the 2,800 miles to Barbados.

Notes and a ticket for a Senagalese Airlines flight found on the boat provided the first pieces of the puzzle:

> I would like to send to my family in Bassada [a town in the interior of Senegal] a sum of money. Please excuse me and goodbye. This is the end of my life in this big Moroccan sea.[30]
>
> I am from Senegal but have been living in Cape Verde for a year. Things are bad. I don't think I will come out of this alive. I need whoever finds me to send this money to my family. Please telephone my friend Ibrahima Drame. Signed Diaw Sounkar Diemi.[31]

*

In the morning hours, radiation from the sun warms the land faster than it warms the sea. The hot air rising from the island pulls the wind from sea to land. So as the sun rises, the island is surrounded on all sides by winds that blow inland from the sea.

Barbados has only two species of plants that are unique to the island: "a common gully shrub *Phyllanthus andersonii* sometimes called broom, and a rare slender climber; *Metastelma barbadense*, which has no common name." The rest of the nearly three thousand varieties of plants came from across the water—some borne by ships and violently cultivated, and others carried by forces of nature: "[In Barbados] flora reach the shores on winds and ocean currents and with the help of birds. In addition many of our wild plants are deliberate introductions which have since become self-seeding and naturalised. It is often said that many of the wild plants of Barbados are exotic weeds."[32] Plants grown from seeds blown across the Antilles were replaced by annihilating fields of sugarcane. These decimated plants, blown by wind and carried by ocean currents and birds, now grow thickly across dirt-hewn paths, on fields grown for grazing, and in gullies carved through coral caves.

A stronger system of winds travels from farther away. Trade winds blow across the Atlantic Ocean to the Caribbean Sea, carrying the weather and, for centuries, the sails of ships from East to West. Dust from the Sahara Desert blows across the Atlantic, moving grain by grain the matter of one continent onto a line of islands on the other side of the ocean. Barbados is the first coast that these particles of dust touch, and during spring, summer, and autumn, the air is full of matter from the Sahel, and the earth is carpeted with its phosphorescence.

1 Anna Lowenhaupt Tsing, "A Feminist Approach to the Anthropocene: Earth Stalked by Man" (Helen Pond McIntyre '48 Lecture, Barnard College, New York, November 10, 2015), https://vimeo.com/149475243.

2 See also the conversation with Henriette Gunkel in this book, especially page 11.

3 Dilip M. Menon, "At the End of Time: Thinking the World from Kochi" (Let's Talk series, Biennale Pavilion, Fort Kochi, March 25, 2017), https://www.youtube.com/watch?v=uwMu3WstQtE.

4 Antonio Benítez-Rojo, *The Repeating Island: The Caribbean and the Postmodern Perspective*, trans. James E. Maraniss, 2nd ed. (Durham, NC: Duke University Press, 1997), 2. Benítez-Rojo distinguishes "Chaos" from "chaos" in order to align his usage with its scientific definition. In this context, Chaos describes random (dis)order, different from the standard usage, which suggests total cacophonous disorder.

5 Benítez-Rojo, 3–4. An "ultima Thule" is a distant unknown region, the extreme limit of travel and discovery.

6 Benítez-Rojo, 8.

7 Walter Benjamin, "Paris, Capital of the Nineteenth Century," in *Reflections: Essays, Aphorisms, Autobiographical Writings*, ed. Peter Demetz, trans. Edmund Jephcott (New York: Schocken Books, 1978), 159.

8 Susan Buck-Morss, "The Flaneur, the Sandwichman and the Whore: The Politics of Loitering," *New German Critique*, no. 39 (Autumn 1986): 108.

9 Elizabeth DeLoughrey, "Ordinary Futures: Interspecies Worldings in the Anthropocene," in *Global Ecologies and the Environmental Humanities: Postcolonial Approaches*, ed. Elizabeth DeLoughrey, Jill Didur, and Anthony Carrigan (New York: Routledge, 2015), 353.

10 Stefan Helmreich, *Alien Ocean: Anthropological Voyages in Microbial Seas* (Berkeley: University of California Press, 2009), 106–44.

11 DeLoughrey, "Ordinary Futures," 365.

12 DeLoughrey, 354.

13 Krista A. Thompson, *An Eye for the Tropics: Tourism, Photography, and Framing the Caribbean Picturesque* (Durham, NC: Duke University Press, 2006), 170–71.

14 Jessica Lehman, "Blue History," *New Inquiry*, February 6, 2017, http://thenewinquiry.com/essays/blue-history/.

15 Lehman, "Blue History."

16 See Joseph M. Prospero and Olga L. Mayol-Bracero, "Understanding the Transport and Impact of African Dust on the Caribbean Basin," *Bulletin of the American Meteorological Society* 94, no. 9 (2013): 1329–37; and Joseph M. Prospero, "Saharan Dust Impacts and Climate Change," *Oceanography* 19, no. 2 (2006): 60–61.

17 Prospero, "Saharan Dust Impacts," 61.

18 Prospero and Mayol-Bracero, "African Dust on the Caribbean Basin," 1331.

19 Prospero, "Saharan Dust Impacts," 60.

20 Georges Bataille, "Dust," in *Encyclopaedia Acephalica*, ed. Alastair Brotchie, trans. Iain White (London: Atlas Press, 1995), 423.

21 Benítez-Rojo, *The Repeating Island*, 3.

22 Kathryn Yusoff, "Geologic Life: Prehistory, Climate, Futures, or Do Fossils Dream of Geologic Life" (unpublished manuscript, April 2012), 11, https://eprints.lancs.ac.uk/id/eprint/73620/1/GeologicLife_April2012_yusoff.pdf.

23 Yusoff, 7.

24 Yusoff, 5.

25 Lindsey Dillon and Julie Sze, "Police Power and Particulate Matters: Environmental Justice and the Spatialities of In/securities in U.S. Cities," *English Language Notes* 54, no. 2 (Fall/Winter 2016): 14.

26 Dillon and Sze, 19.

27 Nicholas Mirzoeff, "Below the Water: Black Lives Matter and Revolutionary Time," *e-flux journal*, no. 79 (February 2017), https://www.e-flux.com/journal/79/94164/below-the-water-black-lives-matter-and-revolutionary-time/.

28 DeLoughrey, "Ordinary Worlds," 358.

29 DeLoughrey, 359.

30 A note found onboard, as reported in the Barbadian newspaper the *Daily Nation*, quoted in Giles Tremlett, "After Four Months at Sea, Ghost Ship with 11 Petrified Corpses Washes Up in Barbados," *Guardian*, May 29, 2016, https://www.theguardian.com/world/2006/may/29/gilestremlett.mainsection.

31 A note found onboard, as reported in *El País*, quoted in Tremlett.

32 Sean Carrington, *Wild Plants of Barbados* (Oxford: Macmillan Caribbean, 2007), 1.

ALIEN TIME: BEING IN VERTIGO

HENRIETTE GUNKEL

> But can we escape becoming dizzy? And who can affirm that vertigo does not haunt the whole of existence?
> —Frantz Fanon, *The Wretched of the Earth*

I.

In Octavia E. Butler's 1979 novel *Kindred*, the first-person narrator, Dana Franklin, a twenty-six-year-old African American woman, is taken on a journey across space and time: from Altadena near Los Angeles in 1976 to the antebellum South in the early 1800s—on the Weylin plantation near Easton, Maryland, where thirty-eight people are enslaved. Dana is forced to travel into her own ancestral past by Rufus Weylin, the son of the plantation owner, who later becomes a slave owner himself. He is her white "several times great grandfather,"[1] who visualizes Dana every time his life is in danger, including as a child when he nearly drowns in a river, and in his mid-twenties, drunk and lying face down in the mud. Each time she is sent back in time, Dana must save Rufus's life—despite the terror that he embodies for her (her status on the plantation is that of a slave). This challenges a typical science-fiction time-travel trope: that one can threaten one's own present and future existence by intervening in the past. For in this case, if Dana *doesn't* intervene, Rufus's daughter Hagar—Dana's great-grandmother, conceived from a forced sexual relationship between Rufus and Alice, a "born free" whom Rufus had enslaved—will not be born, and neither will Dana. However, the moment Hagar is born, and the survival of her lineage guaranteed—as well as the "'future increase' (expanded property-holdings) for the master," as Saidiya Hartman puts it[2]—Dana refuses the obligation to keep Rufus alive, and kills him: "I could feel the knife in my hand, still slippery with perspiration. A slave was a slave. Anything could be done to her. And Rufus was Rufus—erratic, alternately generous and vicious. I could accept him as my ancestor, my younger brother, my friend, but not as my master, and not as my lover. [...] I pulled the knife free of him somehow, raised it, and brought it down again into his back. This time he only grunted. He collapsed across me, somehow still alive, still holding my arm."[3]

Dana's abductions across time and space begin in the year of the United States Bicentennial, the two hundredth anniversary of the adoption of the Declaration of Independence, which is also the year Dana moves into a new apartment with her white husband, Kevin.[4] Dana experiences this involuntary time travel, this transversality, as frightening, as a *feeling* that Butler describes in visual terms: the dizziness that announces the journey quickly turns to nausea, blurred vision, and the darkening of her immediate surroundings. This leads to the dissolution of a presumably stable ground and of the space and people around her, followed by the appearance of another space and different people.[5] The blurring of vision and the subsequent sense of free fall, a spatial movement implicit in the narrative of abduction, is particularly interesting in the context of visual cultures.

"Imagine you are falling. But there is no ground," prompts Hito Steyerl in her 2011 exploration of verticality and vertical worlds in entertainment and military images, and the underlying transformation of surveillance and targeting technology.[6] This view from above, she argues, results in the loss of a horizon—namely, a loss of that which has the sensorial function of producing a stable position and sense of orientation for the observer, as well as a relatively ordered sense of temporality. If the horizon is an artificial device that offers the illusion of stability in an unstable situation, then a vertical perspective shatters this stability—and holds the potential to shatter the illusory "objective," central, linear perspective of the colonial sovereign as well as a linear notion of time and its projection of a calculable future: "As linear perspective began to tumble down with the sinking bodies of slaves thrown into the ocean, for many people today the simulated grounds of aerial imagery provide an illusionary tool of orientation in a condition in which the horizons have, in fact, been shattered. Time is out of joint and we no longer know whether we are objects or subjects as we spiral down in an imperceptible free fall."[7]

Steyerl refers here not only to aerial images produced by drones and Google Maps but also to J. M. W. Turner's painting *Slavers Throwing Overboard the Dead and Dying, Typhoon Coming On* (1840),[8] in which the horizon is tilted, troubled, and blurred and the viewer has lost their stable, colonial position. Turner's image visualizes the slave ship *Zong*, which in 1781 was en route to the Caribbean with more than four hundred captive Africans on board. Body parts, some in shackles, are painted in the liquid foreground, remaining in sight of the ship, effectively referencing the captain's command that his crew jettison 130 Africans overboard in a scheme to claim insurance money. In *Poetics of Relation* (1990), Édouard Glissant also evokes this most profound loss of bearings when he asks us to imagine life on board a slave ship: "Two hundred human beings crammed into a space barely capable of containing a third of them. Imagine vomit, naked flesh, swarming lice, the dead slumped, the dying crouched. Imagine, if you can, the swirling red of mounting to the deck, the ramp they climbed, the black sun on the horizon, *vertigo*, this dizzying sun plastered to the waves."[9]

"Water is an element which remembers the dead."[10] In her book *In the Wake: On Blackness and Being* (2016), Christina Sharpe develops this idea of memorialization by water, arguing that due to how "nutrients cycle through the ocean [...], the atoms of those people who were thrown overboard are out there in the ocean even today."[11] She calls the time it takes for a substance to enter and leave the ocean "residence time," a concept she developed in relation to her research on whale falls: "There have been studies done on whales that have died and have sunk to the seafloor. These studies show that within a few days the whales' bodies are picked almost clean by benthic organisms—those organisms that live on the seafloor. [...] It is most likely that a human body would not make it to the seafloor intact. What happened to the bodies? By which I mean, what happened to the components of their bodies in salt water?"[12] During a 2018 talk at Goldsmiths, University of London, Sharpe further noted: "Whale falls specifically create geographic connectivity by creating islands of nutrients that allow for genes to move from one place to another. [... So] if the Middle Passage is an understanding of how blackness gets made, then these fallen bodies create connectivity throughout the entire diaspora of a shared experience of blackness, thus spatially uniting the diaspora, even across oceans."[13] This sense of deep geologic time, or residence time, brings the depths of the sea into focus and connects whale falls to the notion of free fall that Steyerl evokes in relation to the transformation of surveillance technology and entertainment imageries. Simultaneously, the afterlife of the Middle Passage is linked to a conceptualization of diaspora and current modes of (illegalized) migration, particularly, and precariously, in and around the Mediterranean Sea.

The free fall in *Kindred* appears as a form of montage. There is the dizziness here and the new space and people there, as if there is no in-between, as if Butler is performing a narrative cut: "Then the walls around me and the bed beneath me vanished. I lay sprawled on the ground under a tree."[14] The temporality that emerges from this narrative cut or montage—which, as Steyerl argues, is a "perfect device for destabilizing the observer's perspective and breaking down linear time"[15]—is perceived as "alien time" by Dana, a time of instability, insecurity, and dehumanization that she experiences as a constant threat and ongoing horror, and that impacts the supposedly stable present. This alien time is also perceived and inhabited differently from the time of her present: "I'd gone for nearly two months and come back yesterday—the same day I left home. Nothing was real."[16] This supposedly subjective experience is recognizable through her associates of the past: while Dana remains twenty-six throughout the novel, people of the past grow older.

Dana's return to her present, to the home she just moved into with Kevin, is experienced similarly through intense feeling—panic for her own life, fear of death, and fear for her future existence. Dana reasons, "Then, Rufus's fear of death calls me to him, and my own fear of death sends me home"[17]—a fear that she tries to control, at one point cutting her own wrists in order to get back home. Dana eventually frees herself from being pulled back in time, when she kills Rufus—at a great loss, namely, of her arm, which Rufus was holding when he collapsed across her. This loss doesn't indicate a return to the normative experience of time, where the past/alien time is laid to rest in the aftermath of the event. Rather, it points to the realization that this alien time remains forever part of Dana:

> Something harder and stronger than Rufus's hand clamped down on my arm, squeezing it, stiffening it, pressing into it—painlessly, at first—melting into it, meshing with it as though somehow my arm were being absorbed into something. Something cold and nonliving. Something… paint, plaster, wood—a wall. The wall of my living room. I was back home—in my own house, in my own time. But I was still caught somehow, joined to the wall as though my arm were growing out of it—or growing into it. […] I looked at the spot where flesh joined with plaster, stared at it uncomprehending. It was the exact spot Rufus's finger had grasped. I pulled my arm toward me, pulled hard. And suddenly, there was an avalanche of pain, red impossible agony! And I screamed and screamed.[18]

The narrative cut and its lack of an in-between space—the move from one time zone to the next without any break—points to what Sharpe understands as being "in the wake," which she describes as to "occupy and to be occupied by the continuous and changing present of slavery's as yet unresolved unfolding."[19] Being in the wake of slavery, then, constitutes an understanding of Black subjectivity as marked by the violent disorientations of a state of ongoing vertigo. As articulated by Zakiyyah Iman Jackson in 2016, in her elaboration of vertigo in the context of planetary anti-blackness, it is a "sense of unhinged reality, a communion with death and that realm which exceeds life."[20] Or in the words of Fanon: "But can we escape becoming dizzy? And who can affirm that vertigo does not haunt the whole of existence?"[21]

This sense of the unfinished project of emancipation is operative in *Kindred.* Each time Dana is abducted into the past, the longer her experiences there last—time *stretches*—and the less distance she is able to establish between her different temporal experiences: "I wasn't getting enough time for myself. Once—God knows how long ago—I had worried that I was keeping too much distance between myself and this alien time. Now, there was no distance at all. When had I stopped acting? Why had I stopped?"[22] What Dana calls alien time becomes part of her, overtaking her temporal sense of what constitutes the real—Mark Fisher calls this a "time-slip" in his 2013 exploration of Afrofuturism as hauntology. (At one point, Kevin is also caught in it, when he time travels with Dana, then gets separated from her and lost in the past.) Dana turns into the future ghost of slavery, while at the same time, she is haunted in her own present by those she haunts, another temporal slip that Fisher calls "the looped time of Afrofuturist trauma."[23] So what begins as a typical time-travel trope—suggesting that anyone who lives in the afterlife of transatlantic slavery is a time traveler and that time travel is a different approach to seeing and experiencing the world—becomes the spectral haunting of another time in the present, coexisting in the now. In *Kindred*'s nonconsensual spatiotemporal movement, in this looped time of Afrofuturist trauma, time is out of joint. For Fisher, with reference to Jacques Derrida, this points to the two temporal pulls within hauntology: the pull of the *no longer*, "which is still effective as a virtuality (the traumatic 'compulsion to repeat,' a structure that repeats, a fatal pattern)," and the *not yet*, "which is already effective in the virtual (an attractor, an anticipation shaping current behaviour)."[24]

II.

"Hauntology is a political gesture: a sign that the dead will not be silenced."[25] This political gesture is also evoked in the multimedia work and site-specific installations of Johannesburg-based artist Kitso Lynn Lelliott that form part of her larger research project *South Atlantic Hauntings: Geographies of Memory, Ancestralities and Re-memberings* (2013–ongoing). The ongoing work makes visible the simultaneous presence and absence of elided histories, experiences, and regimes of thought through the figure of the specter. Following Gary Simmons's question of what it means "to conceive of oneself as a giver of shape to ghosts,"[26] and by entering what Tavia Nyong'o, in his exploration of necropolitics, performance art, and Deleuzian negativity, calls the "crypt of blackness,"[27] Lelliott conjures up haunted landscapes, populated by ghosts to whom she gives shape and who give shape to her. These processes of becoming are suggested by the title of one of her video works: *I was her and she was me and those we might become* (2016). Her body, *a* body, takes shape, multiplies itself, and forms intimate and uncanny encounters with the presences of Black women who came before her: for example, Alzire, a young woman from Suriname who was reportedly given as a present to Wilhelmine of Bayreuth and worked in her court in the mid-eighteenth century;[28] or Margaret Garner (Toni Morrison refers to her life in the novel *Beloved*), who killed her own daughter in 1856 to save her from the horror of slavery. Lelliott's audiovisual and performative use of shape-shifting within contexts of time travel as a historical, archival method offers viewers an intimate sense of relations unfolding across time and space, and the recognition of "our" ancestors, who Lelliott understands to be walking among "us," as we approach or enact the future as they might have envisioned it.[29] Pulled toward places marked by the collective trauma of slavery as the founding moment of modernity—historical places that provide an understanding of how blackness is made, to return to Sharpe's argument: the Atlantic, Bahia, Accra, Dakar, Bayreuth—Lelliott makes visible the traces that

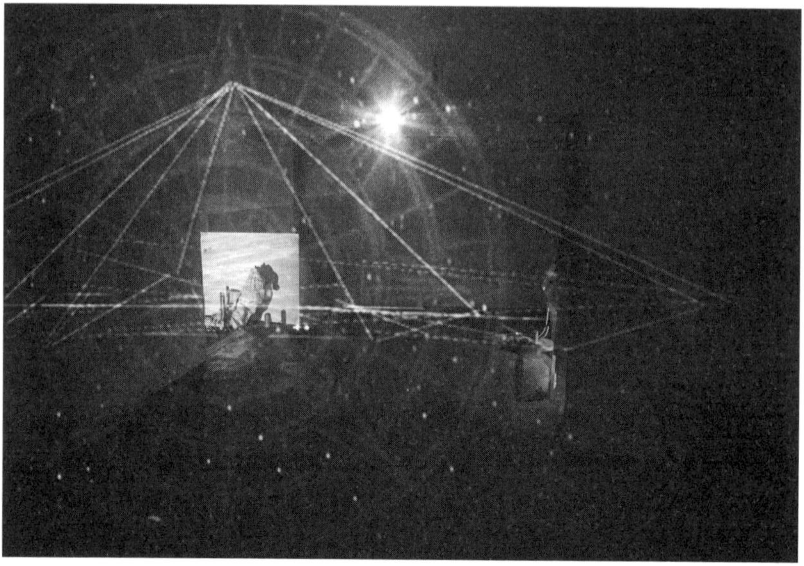

KITSO LYNN LELLIOTT, *I WAS HER AND SHE WAS ME AND THOSE WE MIGHT BECOME*, 2016. INSTALLATION VIEW. PHOTO: LAUREN MULLIGAN. COURTESY OF THE ARTIST

ephemeral, ghostly figures have left in each. By working with cosmological diagramming and a reoccurring camera movement from earth to sky, Lelliott simultaneously takes us into outer space, to the stars and to the moon, and hence to deep space-times, different epistemological spaces, and alternative worlds.

Lelliott seems to avoid showing her works individually, rather placing them in relation to her other works; her films and installations make references to each other, "offering fragments of wholes that fall short just on the margin of coming fully into being," as Layla Leiman writes.[30] In the film *Fungible Things* (2015), for example, the ghost, *a* ghost, appears in an oval frame. This seems to imply that the viewer is looking at a historical image, one that reflects back on the viewer but also on what lies between the viewer and the specter: sugarcane, tobacco, cotton, and rice; objects of colonial commerce, commodities that were shipped alongside

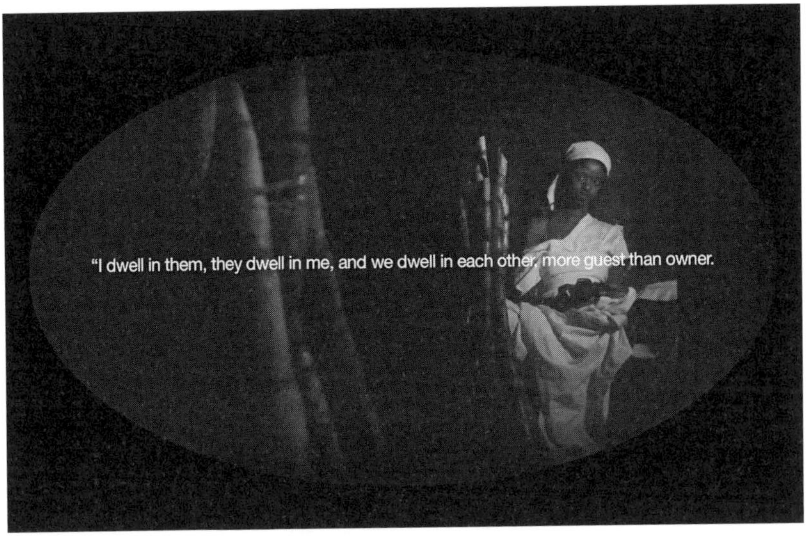

STILL FROM KITSO LYNN LELLIOTT, *FUNGIBLE THINGS*, 2015. COURTESY OF THE ARTIST

captive people, reminding the viewer that enslaved people were themselves considered fungible objects. Ian Baucom refers to this as "the Atlantic cycle of capital accumulation."[31] In Lelliott's work, the objects are mirrored, and hence doubled; the specter holds a camera in her hands, a technology of her future, of this/our time, which seems to enhance the power of the ghost and, to reference Derrida, her ability to haunt us. The ghost is thus inscribed with a relational capacity—an active interrogative agency even—that was denied to her in the processes of "social negation" that, Orlando Patterson argues, positioned the enslaved within contexts of white supremacy as less than human.[32] Fungibility, then, marks not only the objects between the viewer and the frame/mirror, but also the very body that returns the viewer's gaze. As Derrida puts it, "The specter is not simply someone we see coming back, it is someone by whom we feel ourselves watched, observed, surveyed."[33] The different fungible objects of consumption that came before us continue to define any form of relations. In the video, they are therefore introduced consecutively, allowing the viewer to meditate on each, divided by blackouts and parts of a quote by postcolonial thinker and filmmaker Trinh T. Minh-ha, which brings us, yet again, to the looped time of Afrofuturist trauma: "I dwell in them, they dwell in me, and we dwell in each other, more guest than owner. My story, no doubt, is me, but it is also, no doubt, older than me. [...] No end, no middle, no beginning; no start, no stop, no progression; neither backwards not forward, only a stream that flows into another stream, an open sea."[34]

These lines leave traces in Lelliott's video *My story no doubt is me / Older than me* (2015), in which the specter invoked in *Fungible Things* reappears. Here the camera is focused on the backyard of a building on Brazil Road in Jamestown, a neighborhood in Accra, and captures everyday scenes: women doing laundry and fetching water, children playing. As the film unfolds, people seem to vanish from the camera's lens, which is fixed in one position with a clear horizon (the stable position is challenged here not by the loss of horizon but by the emphasis on it), while the specter of *Fungible Things* and other ghosts find ways of making themselves seen. They appear and disappear, multiply, pause, and move around. The ephemeral presences and the traces that their movements leave behind point to alternative spaces in which different regimes of "the real" operate, visualized in the language of a diagram, which connects the spatial and temporal movements of the different specters to one point in the sky, to a specter of the specters, a kind of singular meta-ghost[35]—a meta-ghost who seems to be the origin of everything as well as the past of everything, and appears at one point as a cosmological principle and then disappears again, alongside other figures. Such figures, to name a few, include an animated dancing couple, an ancient Mesopotamian sky chart as a representation of Indigenous cosmologies, other visual imageries of the celestial realms, an old compass, Sankofa as an alternative understanding of time,[36] and identifiers of Cape Coast Castle, Elmina Castle, and the Slave River—which seem to highlight the continuous commerce attached to these historical sites of slavery. At one point in the video, the backyard disappears and the diagram is projected onto the sky, bringing the different bodies that inhabit the sky into focus: human, machine, planetary, spectral, ancestral. The bodies of stars, as specters or extraterrestrial bodies light-years away, might reach us as time travelers, often becoming visible to us only after they have ceased to exist. In this way, the work seems to suggest that light itself becomes spectral, and that in constellations we can find valuable information.

Lelliott's video *Sankofa 1* (2016), which is set in conversation with *My story no doubt is me*, further emphasizes the richness of thinking of bodies as stars. Here the focus is entirely on the extraterrestrial: the Mesopotamian map, Sankofa, Polynesian navigation charts, and admission tickets to key sites in Ghana reappear as means of thinking through the history of slavery, and animal figures, comprised of stars, emerge as visualizations of southern African folktales and astronomical lore.[37] One image that is repeated and animated toward the end of the video is the figure of a girl throwing embers from a fire into the sky, which created the Milky Way, and by extension the universe.[38] Other elements include star maps and a brass sun pendant made by the Dogon people in Mali, who understand themselves as descendants of the star Sirius B. The inclusion of such imagery pays homage to the fact that the Dogon were able to correctly identify and reference Sirius B long before any Western technical device could capture it (the star was only photographed, and hence its existence "proved," in the 1970s).[39] Here the sky becomes a dwelling place for all divine beings and spirits of the dead as well as for the living; different forms of knowledge, histories, and mythologies merge, and interspecies connections are formed.[40] Further, a baobab tree, featured in many of Lelliott's works, links the more abstract deep space-time to deep geologic time; the tree is very old and yet still alive. Thus, like the specters, it brings together different epochs.[41]

Lelliott's work presents what Baucom, referencing Glissant's *Poetics of Relation*, calls "geopolitical forms of being in the world" through their unfolding of alien time and the traces left by the objects and figures that inhabit her videos and spaces.[42] We could conceptualize these traces across time and space, connected via the universe and the Atlantic, in Glissant's terms, as a posture or relational politics of errancy, which is "not so much to be mistaken, as to be in transit, to be in imaginative flight across the world"—a flight that also finds its way into Sharpe's understanding of the wake. For Glissant, the Black Atlantic world is an experience of living in relation, an "oceanic feeling," one could argue, that Sigmund Freud, referencing Romain Rolland, describes as "this feeling of indissoluble connection, of belonging inseparably to the external world as a whole."[43] In Lelliott's work, this is particularly emphasized in another video titled *Transatlantic Saudades* (2013), which seems to connect the different places she is drawn to, while simultaneously linking the Black Atlantic to the extraterrestrial—both key sites of Afrofuturist contemplation.

Transatlantic Saudades evokes what Baucom, in response to Derek Walcott's poem "The Sea Is History," calls the "unsettled ancestor[s] of a living Atlantic citizenry."[44] Lelliott shot the piece while on a residency in Bahia on the coast of Brazil, part of the littoral zone that marked saltwater slavery.[45] It cites the poem "Transatlantic Saudades," written by Croatian artist Maja Klarić while on the same residency as Lelliott: "At dusk, before the rain / In a deserted corner of the beach / Facing the insurmountable amount of water / Between my island and yours / Never again conquered distance / Between continents that split long ago / Like round people in Plato / I am as lost as the other half / And as alone as the string of a berimbau."[46] Baucom's living Atlantic citizenry includes the Detroit techno duo Drexciya,[47] who, as set out in the liner notes of their album *The Quest* (1997), understood themselves as offspring of pregnant Africans who were thrown or jumped overboard and moved from the amniotic fluid of the womb to the ocean water, and were thus able to adapt and build an underwater city with the same name: "Are Drexciyans water breathing, aquatically mutated descendants of those unfortunate victims of human greed? Have they been spared by God to teach us or terrorize us? […] Do they walk among us? […] What is their Quest?"[48]

Transporting oneself into the realm of the future—a not-yet, a world-to-come—by simultaneously moving backward in (deep) time through the unfolding of relations breaks with both linear and cyclical time. Similar to the spectral, time becomes malleable in Lelliott's work. This becomes particularly evident in *I was her and she was me*, in which Lelliott proposes a multilayered treatment of time. As specters dress up in garments of the past, different temporalities are employed and blend into each other in these partly overlapping, partly parallel or consecutive movements: time is slowed (the number of frames per second dramatically increased to present a time-lapse motion), and time is sped-up (the number of frames per second reduced), yet a normative understanding of time is also presented. As a result, these performances of putting on and taking off the clothing of different times and spaces create a constant sense of being(s) out of place. Or, to put it differently, in some instances, these disjointed temporal movements suggest that the specters own the clothes, while in others, they seem to be fighting against them. But also suggested is the persistence of these specters through each and every moment of time. This raises a question. If—similar to the baobab tree—they have remained present, from the beginning of slavery until today, how do they perceive our (human) time, our (human) lifetime? What is the temporal rhythm to which the specter adheres?

In *I was her and she was me*, time doesn't correlate, akin to the alien time that Dana experiences as the ghost of the past's future, a past not yet past, a past in the present, an accumulation of time, as Lelliott understands it, following Baucom, who argues that time does not pass; rather, time accumulates, abandoning "the temporal schemes of its progressive philosophy of history."[49] Baucom speaks of an accumulation of time that is not "just an abstract measure of time endlessly and indifferently adding up, but, rather, a modern order of time, the time of modernity: which piles up from an exceptional historical catastrophe," the slave trade.[50] Time as something constantly progressing is challenged in Lelliott's work. She points to a past that accumulates, and accumulation exists in her work as unending, and unavoidable: the looped time of Afrofuturist trauma. No end, no middle, no beginning; no start, no stop, no progression; neither backward nor forward, only a stream that flows into another stream, an open sea.

Like Dana in *Kindred*, Lelliott's multimedia work follows a pull from the past through a sense of being in community through and by the continued vulnerability of simultaneous immersion in the no longer and the not yet; it makes visible that which is neither present nor absent, neither dead nor alive. As Lelliott put it in a 2017 talk at the University of Bayreuth, directly quoting Saidiya Hartman: "I too live in the time of slavery—by which I mean I am living in the future created by it."[51] Thus, Lelliott's work points to what Keguro Macharia, in his homage to Audre Lorde, understands as "survival towards freedom," which is a matter of "holding on to those who did not survive, to those not surviving, to those who might not survive."[52] She seems to ask: How will we understand a future in which most of the community will not join us? How will we enact the present-futures they imagined and do the same for those who follow?[53] In thinking about Black futures as a practice that pulls from the past to imagine a future-as-difference,[54] Lelliott's work seems to take this haunting as a provocation to explore a collectivity in speculation, a collectivity to come. Guided by Avery Gordon's call to "remember ghostly histories and their traces in our lives,"[55] Lelliott's work engages with a sense of being in community, via Black death and erasure, that takes performance art, action, and the body seriously.

III.

Lelliott's looped multimedia works, like Butler's writing, evoke the specters of the Atlantic abyss and the ghosts of transatlantic slavery, providing a sense of the endurance and accumulation that also characterize Glissant's geopoetics. Here ghostly figures embody "both a geography of history and a form of time, a type of contemporaneity, a complex, enigmatic, Atlantic 'now.'"[56] In so doing, Lelliott's work also introduces the viewer to rituals and systems of time that predate and are alternative to the time of modernity—and here it is important to remember that Greenwich Mean Time was only introduced as the global time standard in 1884, the same year of the Berlin Conference, during which European colonial powers divided the African continent among themselves and set many of the national borders that continue to exist today.[57] Lelliott makes reference to alternative temporal concepts, rhythms, and senses via the stars, the moon, Dogon and Xan mythology, and various nonlinear temporal media techniques,[58] to name just a few. These point toward different systems of thought and ways of knowing, and, linked to this, possibly non-vertiginous ways of being in and experiencing this world.

Lelliott's *South Atlantic Hauntings* and Butler's *Kindred* resist the classic science-fiction understanding of time travel in which predominantly white male subjects, as voluntary, consensual voyagers through time, decide to conquer time and space, thus sustaining rather than challenging a normative understanding of temporality as defined by the three "dimensions" of past, present, and future. Despite Christine Y. Kim's argument that time travel is about providing a "sense of perception beyond the linear limitation of body, time and space,"[59] classic science-fiction narratives and futurist models that overcome boundaries imparted by the physical world tend to adhere to current cultural norms and sociopolitical frameworks. In *The Time Machine* (1895), for example, H. G. Wells presents a white (male) fantasy of speed and technology in which it is possible to control the future by moving away from the past. In so doing, it encourages a continued linear and normative understanding of time. The time travel that Butler's and Lelliott's works enact is not actualized through some technical device, a high-speed something, but rather through the body itself and its movements between different time zones or dimensions. Technology comes into their works through the racialized body, which is therefore implicated in and becomes the vessel for psychological, traumatic, historical, vertical movement across time and space.

In the afterlife of transatlantic slavery, time travel is part of being "in the wake," and thus becomes more than a historical method: it becomes a method of memory work, of excavating the past, of making visible what lies (undocumented) in the past, a method that includes not only archival work but also—due to the voids in the archive—critical fabulation.[60] In both Butler's and Lelliott's work, the tension between the method and experience of time travel and spectral time becomes apparent (the dual temporal movement implied in the idea of haunting, in the idea of how the past invades and forms the self; the temporal movement of the no longer and the not yet, both of which are already effectively in the virtual). Alien time—which in Butler is considered a strange time of the past, accessed through the sense of vertigo caused by forced movement across time and space—then becomes part of the "Atlantic now" as an understanding of temporal accumulation. This coexistence of spectral time and alien time points to the enriching critical capacity of visual culture in the context of time travel.

Thus, time travel in the context of alien time is not only directed toward the past and concerned with memory and/or counter-memory but operates simultaneously as an anticipation of a different world to come that operates beyond a Eurocentric, white frame of reference. This temporally disjointed movement, and the political implications at stake therein, aligns with what Sharpe calls "wake work" to understand how something may be memorialized when it is still unfolding—very much like chattel slavery and its afterlives within the present, an issue that both Lelliott and Butler explore with commitment. Sharpe writes: "Wakes are processes; through them we think about the dead and about our relations to them; they are rituals through which to enact grief and memory."[61] This also corresponds with the political responsibility that, for Derrida, the spectral brings to the fore. What the spectral alerts us to in the context of alien time, then, is the need for justice for those who are not or no longer there, as well as for those yet to come.

Both Butler's *Kindred* and Lelliott's artistic practice provide this mode of simultaneously inhabiting and rupturing slavery's afterlives in order to imagine otherwise, while remaining attentive to the unfinished conversation of emancipation—a conversation that remains urgent today, as the Far Right and white supremacy are once again gaining momentum. Here in Europe, we are dishearteningly far from continuing this emancipatory conversation in a meaningful, let alone applicable and effective way. Since 2006, the artist Banu Cennetoğlu has been continually publishing and updating *The List*, which documents the names of more than 35,000 migrants and refugees who have died within or at the borders of Europe since 1993.[62] *The sea is history. The past that is not the past reappears, always, to rupture the present.*

1 Octavia E. Butler, *Kindred* (Boston: Beacon Press, 2004), 28.
2 Saidiya Hartman, "The Belly of the World: A Note on Black Women's Labors," *Souls* 18, no. 1 (June 2016): 166. In her exploration of Black women's sexual and reproductive labor in the context of slavery and its afterlife, Hartman writes: "The plantation is the belly of the world. *Partus sequitur ventrem*—the child follows the belly."
3 Butler, *Kindred*, 260.
4 In their seminal reading of *Kindred*, which traces the social and economic implications of the Plantationocene to realities of debt (and its obligations) in the United States today, Paula Chakravartty and Denise Ferreira da Silva argue that the characters' moving in together further means entering the "racial logic of global capitalism": "We highlight how the subprime crisis facilitated this exacting of profits from places to persons produced as unsuitable economic subjects. We do so by shifting the focus on to how conquest and slavery, along with the postcolonial apparatus of raciality, produce places and persons marked by a debt that—like Dana's to her slave-owner ancestor—cannot be settled even with death." They continue: "What is it about blackness and Latinidad that turns one's house (roof, protection, and aspiration) and shelter into a death trap?" Chakravartty and Ferreira da Silva, "Accumulation, Dispossession, and Debt: The Racial Logic of Global Capitalism—An Introduction," *American Quarterly* 64, no. 3 (September 2012): 365, 367.
5 Dana's first abduction through time and space is described as follows: "I bent to push [Kevin] another box full [of books], then straightened quickly as I began to feel dizzy, nauseated. The room seemed to blur and darken around me. I stayed on my feet for a moment holding on to a bookcase and wondering what was wrong, then finally, I collapsed on my knees. I heard Kevin make a wordless sound of surprise, heard him ask, 'What happened?' I raised my head and discovered that I could not focus on him. 'Something is wrong with me,' I gasped. I heard him move toward me, saw a blur of gray pants and blue shirt. Then, just before he would have touched me, he vanished. The house, the books, everything vanished. Suddenly, I was outdoors kneeling on the ground beneath trees. I was in a green place. I was at the edge of woods. Before me was a wide tranquil river, and near the middle of that river was a child splashing, screaming… Drowning!" Butler, *Kindred*, 13.
6 Hito Steyerl, "In Free Fall: A Thought Experiment on Vertical Perspective," *e-flux journal*, no. 24 (April 2011), https://www.e-flux.com/journal/24/67860/in-free-fall-a-thought-experiment-on-vertical-perspective/.
7 Steyerl, "In Free Fall." The potentiality of a sense of instability through free fall in order to challenge normative positions and understandings of being in the world (thus removing it from the exclusive framework/experience of subjection) is also taken up by Diann Bauer, one of the members of Laboria Cuboniks, in her first visual introduction to the Xenofeminist Manifesto, produced for a seminar she was invited to. It opens with the declaration that "ours is a world in vertigo" and an image of an astronaut in free fall, escaping gravity. This is a free fall that allows for a politics of alienation ("alienation is the labour of freedom's construction") that, as Laboria Cuboniks argue, seems necessary to construct the world otherwise; that allows us to understand nothing "as fixed, permanent, or 'given'—neither material conditions nor social forms. XF mutates, navigates and probes every horizon." Laboria Cuboniks, *Xenofeminism: A Politics for Alienation*, 2015, http://laboriacuboniks.net.
8 See also the conversation with Ayesha Hameed in this book, especially pages 17–19.
9 Édouard Glissant, *Poetics of Relation*, trans. Betsy Wing (Ann Arbor: University of Michigan Press, 1997), 5–6 (emphasis added).
10 Elizabeth DeLoughrey, "Heavy Waters: Waste and Atlantic Modernity," *Publications of the Modern Language Association of America* 125, no. 3 (2010): 704.
11 Christina Sharpe, *In the Wake: On Blackness and Being* (Durham, NC: Duke University Press, 2016), 40–41.

12 Sharpe, 40. The very term "residence time" seems to already connote something hauntological. See also, in this book, Ayesha Hameed's essay, especially pages 17–19, and our conversation, pages 18, 49, and 61–62.

13 Christina Sharpe, "Black. Still. Life." (lecture, Goldsmiths, University of London, May 17, 2018).

14 Butler, *Kindred*, 58. This form of montage becomes even more apparent in Damian Duffy and John Jennings's 2018 graphic novel adaptation of *Kindred*, in which each sentence of this passage is turned into an image.

15 Steyerl, "In Free Fall."

16 Butler, *Kindred*, 115.

17 Butler, 50.

18 Butler, 260–61.

19 Sharpe, *In the Wake*, 13–14. For Sharpe, "the wake" has several meanings: "the keeping watch with the dead, the path of the ship, a consequence of something, in the line of flight and/or sight, awakening, and consciousness" (17–18).

20 Zakiyyah Iman Jackson, "Sense of Things," *Catalyst: Feminism, Theory, Technoscience* 2, no. 2 (2016): 23.

21 Frantz Fanon, *The Wretched of the Earth*, trans. Constance Farrington (New York: Grove Press, 1968), 253. Frank B. Wilderson III importantly draws the distinction between *subjective vertigo* ("a dizzying sense that one is moving or spinning in an otherwise stationary world, a vertigo brought on by a clash of grossly asymmetrical forces") and *objective vertigo* ("the sensation that one is not simply spinning in an otherwise stable environment, that one's environment is perpetually unhinged stems from a relationship to violence that cannot be analogized"). For him, Black life takes place at the crossroads where vertigos meet, at the intersection of performative and structural violence, which, in effect, provides us with an understanding of blackness as a "life constituted by disorientation rather than a life interrupted by disorientation." Wilderson, "The Vengeance of Vertigo: Aphasia and Abjection in the Political Trials of Black Insurgents," *InTensions*, no. 5 (Fall/Winter 2011), http://www.yorku.ca/intent/issue5/articles/frankbwildersoniii.php.

22 Butler, *Kindred*, 220.

23 Mark Fisher, "The Metaphysics of Crackle: Afrofuturism and Hauntology," *Dancecult: Journal of Electronic Dance Music Culture* 5, no. 2 (November 2013): 51. Fisher develops this notion specifically in relation to *Kindred*: "Projected into the looped time of Afrofuturist trauma, *Kindred*'s Dana becomes 'like a ghost.'" He then quotes Butler's original text: "'Disappeared? You mean like smoke?' Fear crept into his expression. 'Like a ghost?'" before continuing his analysis: "A spectre-from-the-future whose intervention in the past allows that future to happen. The deep, unbearable ache in *Kindred* arises from the horrible realisation that, for contemporary black America, to wish for the erasure of slavery is to call for the erasure of itself. What to do if the precondition of your being is the abduction, murder and rape of your ancestors?"

24 Mark Fisher, "What Is Hauntology?," *Film Quarterly* 66, no. 1 (Fall 2012): 19. For Avery Gordon, haunting provides "an animated state in which a repressed or unresolved social violence is making itself known, [...] those singular yet repetitive instances when home becomes unfamiliar, when your bearings on the world lose direction, when the over-and-done-with comes alive, when what's been in your blind spot comes into view." Gordon, *Ghostly Matters: Haunting and the Sociological Imagination* (Minneapolis: University of Minnesota Press, 2008), xvi.

25 Fisher, "Metaphysics of Crackle," 53.

26 Gordon, *Ghostly Matters*, 93.

27 Tavia Nyong'o, "The Crypt of Blackness: or Assotto Saint with Gilles Deleuze," in *We Travel the Space Ways: Black Imagination, Fragments, and Diffractions*, ed. Henriette Gunkel and kara lynch (Bielefeld: transcript, 2019), 175.

28 There is little information available on the life of Alzire, which points to the gaps in the archive.

29 Here, following Lelliott, I am talking specifically about a "we" and an "us," because I understand Lelliott's work as pointing to a history that is the shared history of each and every one of us, regardless of geopolitical and racialized positioning. In the centering of Black epistemologies and aesthetics, it is important

to acknowledge that the excavation of the past is important to all of us—not in a way that makes whiteness yet again invisible or assigns it a "neutral" position, but by acknowledging how different histories (some visible, some not) define us all, albeit in varying ways. Whiteness is produced by elisions in the archive, and in pointing to the void in the archive it is important to provide an understanding that the histories that are missing are the histories of all of us, and that the different and complex power relations that have formed these histories and experiences are still operating today. See also Gunkel and lynch, *We Travel the Space Ways.*

30 Layla Leiman, "Making Space for the Dream and Poetry in Kitso Lynn Lelliott's Work," *Between 10 and 5*, November 29, 2016, https://10and5.com/2016/11/29/making-space-for-the-dream-and-poetry-in-kitso-lynn-lelliotts-work/.

31 Ian Baucom, *Specters of the Atlantic: Finance Capital, Slavery, and the Philosophy of History* (Durham, NC: Duke University Press, 2005), 80.

32 Orlando Patterson, *Slavery and Social Death: A Comparative Study* (Cambridge, MA: Harvard University Press, 1982), 38.

33 Jacques Derrida, in *Echographies of Television: Filmed Interviews*, trans. Jennifer Bajorek (Cambridge: Polity, 2002), 41.

34 Trinh T. Minh-ha, *Women, Native, Other: Writing Postcoloniality and Feminism* (Bloomington: Indiana University Press, 1989), 123.

35 Similar to the ghost in the mirror in *Fungible Things*, I would argue.

36 In the Ghanaian Adinkra knowledge system, Sankofa is a concept that loosely means one has to look back to where they came from in order to see where they are going.

37 In our conversation in Bayreuth, October 2017, Lelliott pointed out that she was particularly drawn to Tswana and Xam star lore.

38 This moment in the film visualizes Xam star lore, which says that the stars were once people, their ancestors, and identifies the Milky Way as a supernatural footpath across the sky along which the ancestors' spirits walked.

39 Every fifty years—this is how long it takes for Sirius B to complete its orbit—the Dogon celebrate this origin with large-scale festivities.

40 Or as Lelliott put it: "I was thinking through different ways/knowledge systems/epistemes (and also technologies) through which people have conceived of where and how they are in the world/universe, and the diversity of these over vast times and spaces, marking where we are in and amongst the vastness to deep space, time, and multiple ways of conceiving those." Conversation with the author, Bayreuth, October 2017.

41 Baobab trees, native to sub-Saharan Africa, can live to be more than two thousand years old. In the last twelve years, however, a number of the oldest trees have died, which is considered a result of climate change. See, for example, GrrlScientist, "Africa's Oldest Baobab Trees Are Likely Victims of Climate Change," *Forbes*, June 17, 2018, https://www.forbes.com/sites/grrlscientist/2018/06/17/africas-oldest-baobab-trees-are-probably-the-victims-of-climate-change/.

42 Baucom, *Specters of the Atlantic*, 312. The ephemeral presences leave their traces in, and form relations to, different spaces and different videos that are installed in relation to each other and in varying constellations in this ongoing work, alongside a dress or objects of commerce. The backyard in Accra, for example, reappears on a monitor in *Sankofa 1*, a video that brings the celestial to the foreground. The objects of commerce that are between the viewer and the mirror/frame in *Fungible Things* (sugarcane, tobacco, cotton, and rice) found their way into the exhibition "I was her and she was me and those we might become" (2017) at Room Gallery, Johannesburg. Housed in wooden and glass boxes placed on the floor and in proximity to the video work, they form replicas of ordinary boxes that Lelliott worked with in Ghana, themselves objects of commerce. Similarly, the dresses and jewelry in the exhibition's eponymous video refer to the alternative times and places from which the different generations of specters emerge, and allow the viewer to understand the scattering of those lives evoked in the works—for example, the dress installed in Lelliott's work *Alzire of Bayreuth* (2016) resembles a dress most likely worn in Bayreuth at the time.

43 Erika Balsom, *An Oceanic Feeling: Cinema and the Sea* (New Plymouth, New Zealand: Govett-Brewster Art Gallery, 2018), 9. Balsom relates Freud's interpretation of Rollard's notion of "oceanic feeling" as "the sensation of an unbreakable bond between oneself and the outside world. Rather than any autonomy or mastery, oceanic feeling is a quasi-sublime state in which the integrity of the self is lost, or at least compromised, in a sense of limitlessness, unboundedness, and interconnectedness." Reading Freud's idea into the Black Atlantic, in the context of the Anthropocene, the aquatic history of transatlantic slavery, and current modes of migration, Balsom argues that it might allow for a "dispossession of the ego and decentring of the human" and can "serve as a ground of practice of implication, remembrance, and care" (9, 10).

44 Baucom, *Specters of the Atlantic*, 322.

45 The term "saltwater slavery" is borrowed from Stephanie E. Smallwood, *Saltwater Slavery: A Middle Passage from Africa to American Diaspora* (Cambridge, MA: Harvard University Press), 2007.

46 Maja Klarić, "Saudade Transatlântica," Instituto Sacatar, http://www.sacatar.com.br/site/ing/alumni.asp?id=250 (link discontinued, accessed October 21, 2019).

47 See also, in this book, Hameed's text, esp. page 28, and the conversation, page 11.

48 Liner notes of Drexciya, *The Quest*, Submerge, SVE-8, 1997.

49 Baucom, *Specters of the Atlantic*, 311.

50 Baucom, 320. He argues further: "To lay the past to rest thus means not that we should forget it but that we have no choice but to relate it, no choice but to live on within the full knowledge and unending of it. Time does not pass but accumulates. Why? Because what has been begun does not end but endures. Because this fatal Atlantic 'beginning' of the modern is more properly understood as an ending without end. Because history comes to us not only as flash or revelation but piling up. Because this is, not was. Because this is the Atlantic, now. Because all of it is now, it is always now, even for you who never was there" (333).

51 Saidiya Hartman, *Lose Your Mother: A Journey along the Atlantic Slave Route* (New York: Farrar, Straus and Giroux, 2007), 133.

52 Keguro Macharia, "Survival in Audre Lorde," *New Inquiry*, August 25, 2017, https://thenewinquiry.com/blog/survival-in-audre-lorde.

53 kara lynch and I ask these questions in our introduction to *We Travel the Space Ways*, 21–43.

54 Hugh Charles O'Connell distinguishes between the "merely quantitative notion of the future," that is, between a mere passing of time, and the "qualitative notion of the future-as-difference" that he calls futurity. He develops this distinction in a footnote and in relation to Fisher's understanding that "although time continues to pass, there is no radical historical progressiveness or sense of a future outside of the conditions of global late capitalism." O'Connell, "'We Are Change': The Novum as Event in Nnedi Okorafor's *Lagoon*," *Cambridge Journal of Postcolonial Literary Inquiry* 3, no. 3 (2016): 292.

55 Gordon, *Ghostly Matters*, 93.

56 Baucom, *Specters of the Atlantic*, 324.

57 For further discussions on the colonial conceptions of time, see, for example, Bliss Cua Lim, *Translating Time: Cinema, the Fantastic, and Temporal Critique* (Durham, NC: Duke University Press, 2009); Giordano Nanni, *The Colonisation of Time: Ritual, Routine and Resistance in the British Empire* (Manchester: Manchester University Press, 2009); Johannes Fabian, *Time and the Other: How Anthropology Makes Its Object* (New York: Columbia University Press, 2014); and Kevin K. Birth, *Time Blind: Problems in Perceiving Other Temporalities* (London: Palgrave Macmillan, 2017).

58 Alain Resnais and Chris Marker have been particularly influential in the disruption of standard narrative chronology in cinema. See Ed Halter, "Travel Agents: Alain Resnais's *Je t'aime, je t'aime* and the Cinematic Time Machine," *Artforum International*, February 2014, 182–89. In the text "Alienation and Queer Discontent," in *We Travel the Space Ways*, I argue how the use of different temporal strategies in the film *Stories of Our Lives* (2014), by Jim Chuchu and the Nest Collective, leads to different ways of inhabiting space in the context of queerness.

59 Christine Y. Kim, "The Politics of Rupture," in *Philosophy of Time Travel*, ed. Christine Y. Kim (New York: Studio Museum in Harlem, 2007), 19.

60 See Hartman, *Scenes of Subjection*.

61 Sharpe, *In the Wake*, 17. She continues: "If [...] we think the metaphor of the wake in the entirety of its meanings (the keeping watch with the dead, the path of the ship, a consequence of something, in the line of flight and/or sight, awakening, and consciousness) and we join the wake with work in order that we might make the wake and wake work our analytic, we might continue to imagine new ways to live in the wake of slavery, in slavery's afterlives, to survive (and more) the afterlife of property. In short, I mean wake work to be a mode of inhabiting *and* rupturing this episteme with our known lived and un/imaginable lives. With that analytic we might imagine otherwise from what we know *now* in the wake of slavery" (17–18).

62 An interactive online map shows fifteen years of migrant and refugee deaths that occurred en route to Europe or while attempting to stay in Europe: Moriz Buesing, "15 Years Fortress Europe," http://15years.morizbuesing.com. The data was compiled by the Migrants' Files project (http://www.themigrantsfiles.com) and UNITED for Intercultural Action (http://www.unitedagainst refugeedeaths.eu).

BIBLIOGRAPHY

Azoulay, Ariella. *The Civil Contract of Photography.* New York: Zone Books, 2008.

Balsom, Erika. *An Oceanic Feeling: Cinema and the Sea.* New Plymouth, New Zealand: Govett-Brewster Art Gallery, 2018.

Barthes, Roland. *Camera Lucida.* Translated by Richard Howard. New York: Hill & Wang, 1980.

Bataille, Georges. "Dust." In *Encyclopaedia Acephalica,* edited by Alastair Brotchie, translated by Iain White, 42–43. London: Atlas Press, 1995.

Baucom, Ian. *Specters of the Atlantic: Finance Capital, Slavery, and the Philosophy of History.* Durham, NC: Duke University Press, 2005.

Benítez-Rojo, Antonio. *The Repeating Island: The Caribbean and the Postmodern Perspective.* Translated by James E. Maraniss. 2nd ed. Durham, NC: Duke University Press, 1997.

Benjamin, Walter. "Paris, Capital of the Nineteenth Century." In *Reflections: Essays, Aphorisms, Autobiographical Writings,* edited by Peter Demetz, translated by Edmund Jephcott, 146–62. New York: Schocken Books, 1978.

Birth, Kevin K. *Time Blind: Problems in Perceiving Other Temporalities.* London: Palgrave Macmillan, 2017.

Buck-Morss, Susan. "The Flaneur, the Sandwichman and the Whore: The Politics of Loitering." *New German Critique,* no. 39 (Autumn 1986): 99–140.

Butler, Octavia E. *Kindred.* Boston: Beacon Press, 2004.

Butler, Octavia E., Damien Duffy, and John Jennings. *A Graphic Novel Adaptation by Damien Duffy and John Jennings of Octavia E. Butler's "Kindred."* New York: Abrams ComicArts, 2018.

Carrington, Sean. *Wild Plants of Barbados.* Oxford: Macmillan Caribbean, 2007.

Chakravartty, Paula, and Denise Ferreira da Silva. "Accumulation, Dispossession, and Debt: The Racial Logic of Global Capitalism—An Introduction." *American Quarterly* 64, no. 3 (September 2012): 361–85.

Coatman, Anna. "Sondra Perry on Blackness, Gender and Internet Culture," Royal Academy of Arts, March 6, 2018. https://www.royalacademy.org.uk/article/magazine-sondra-perry-typhoon-coming-on-serpentine-galleries.

DeLoughrey, Elizabeth. "Heavy Waters: Waste and Atlantic Modernity." *Publications of the Modern Language Association of America* 125, no. 3 (2010): 703–12.

———. "Ordinary Futures: Interspecies Worldings in the Anthropocene." In *Global Ecologies and the Environmental Humanities: Postcolonial Approaches,* edited by Elizabeth DeLoughrey, Jill Didur, and Anthony Carrigan, 352–72. New York: Routledge, 2015.

Derrida, Jacques, and Bernard Stiegler. *Echographies of Television: Filmed Interviews.* Translated by Jennifer Bajorek. Cambridge: Polity, 2002.

Dillon, Lindsey, and Julie Sze. "Police Power and Particulate Matters: Environmental Justice and the Spatialities of In/securities in U.S. Cities." *English Language Notes* 54, no. 2 (Fall/Winter 2016): 13–23.

Drexciya. *The Quest.* Submerge, SVE-8, 1997. Liner notes.

Eshun, Kodwo. "Further Considerations on Afrofuturism." *CR: The New Centennial Review* 3, no. 2 (2013): 287–302.

Fabian, Johannes. *Time and the Other: How Anthropology Makes Its Object.* New York: Columbia University Press, 2014.

Fanon, Frantz. *The Wretched of the Earth.* Translated by Constance Farrington. New York: Grove Press, 1968.

Fisher, Mark. "The Metaphysics of Crackle: Afrofuturism and Hauntology." *Dancecult: Journal of Electronic Dance Music Culture* 5, no. 2 (November 2013): 42–55.

———. "What Is Hauntology?" *Film Quarterly* 66, no. 1 (Fall 2012): 16–24.

Gebreyesus, Ruth. "Why the Film-Maker behind *Love Is the Message* Is Turning His Lens to Whiteness." *Guardian,* December 11, 2018. https://www.theguardian.com/artanddesign/2018/dec/11/arthur-jafa-video-artist-love-is-the-message.

Gilroy, Paul. *Small Acts: Thoughts on the Politics of Black Cultures.* London: Serpent's Tail, 1994.

Glissant, Édouard. *Poetics of Relation.* Translated by Betsy Wing. Ann Arbor: University of Michigan Press, 1997.

Gordon, Avery F. *Ghostly Matters: Haunting and the Sociological Imagination.* Minneapolis: University of Minnesota Press, 2008.

GrrlScientist. "Africa's Oldest Baobab Trees Are Likely Victims of Climate Change." *Forbes,* June 17, 2018. https://www.forbes.com/sites/grrlscientist/2018/06/17/africas-oldest-baobab-trees-are-probably-the-victims-of-climate-change/#7e205e7a25f4.

Gunkel, Henriette. "Alienation and Queer Discontent." In Gunkel and lynch, *We Travel the Space Ways,* 387–403.

Gunkel, Henriette, Ayesha Hameed, and Simon O'Sullivan, eds. *Futures and Fictions.* London: Repeater Books, 2017.

Gunkel, Henriette, and kara lynch, eds. *We Travel the Space Ways: Black Imagination, Fragments, and Diffractions.* Bielefeld: transcript, 2019.

Halberstam, Jack. "Unbuilding Gender: Trans* Anarchitectures in and beyond the Work of Gordon Matta-Clark." *Places,* October 2018. https://placesjournal.org/article/unbuilding-gender/.

Halter, Ed. "Travel Agents: Alain Resnais's *Je t'aime, je t'aime* and the Cinematic Time Machine." *Artforum International,* February 2014, 182–89.

Hameed, Ayesha. "Black Atlantis." In Gunkel and lynch, *We Travel the Space Ways,* 107–26.

Haraway, Donna. "Anthropocene, Capitalocene, Plantationocene, Chthulucene: Making Kin." *Environmental Humanities* 6, no. 1 (2015): 159–65.

Hartman, Saidiya. "The Belly of the World: A Note on Black Women's Labors." *Souls* 18, no. 1 (June 2016): 166–73.

———. *Lose Your Mother: A Journey along the Atlantic Slave Route.* New York: Farrar, Straus and Giroux, 2007.

———. *Scenes of Subjection: Terror, Slavery, and Self-Making in Nineteenth-Century America.* Oxford: Oxford University Press, 1997.

———. "Venus in Two Acts." *Small Axe,* no. 26 (June 2008): 1–14.

Helmreich, Stefan. *Alien Ocean: Anthropological Voyages in Microbial Seas.* Berkeley: University of California Press, 2009.

Jackson, Zakiyyah Iman. "Sense of Things." *Catalyst: Feminism, Theory, Technoscience* 2, no. 2 (2016): 1–48.

Kim, Christine Y. "The Politics of Rupture." In *Philosophy of Time Travel,* edited by Christine Y. Kim, 17–31. New York: Studio Museum in Harlem, 2007.

Laboria Cuboniks. *Xenofeminism: A Politics for Alienation,* 2015. http://www.laboriacuboniks.net/.

Lehman, Jessica. "Blue History." *New Inquiry,* February 6, 2017. http://thenewinquiry.com/essays/blue-history/.

Leiman, Layla. "Making Space for the Dream and Poetry in Kitso Lynn Lelliott's Work." Interview with Kitso Lynn Lelliott. *Between 10 and 5,* November 29, 2016. http://10and5.com/2016/11/29/making-space-for-the-dream-and-poetry-in-kitso-lynn-lelliotts-work.

Lim, Bliss Cua. *Translating Time: Cinema, the Fantastic, and Temporal Critique.* Durham, NC: Duke University Press, 2009.

Macharia, Keguro. "Survival in Audre Lorde." *New Inquiry,* August 25, 2017. https://thenewinquiry.com/blog/survival-in-audre-lorde.

Marks, Laura U. "Monad, Database, Remix: Manners of Unfolding in *The Last Angel of History.*" *Black Camera* 6, no. 2 (Spring 2015): 112–34.

Menon, Dilip M. "At the End of Time: Thinking the World from Kochi." Let's Talk series, Biennale Pavilion, Fort Kochi. YouTube video, 55:03. Published by Kochi-Muziris Biennale, June 23, 2017. https://www.youtube.com/watch?v=uwMu3WstQtE.

Minh-ha, Trinh. *Women, Native, Other: Writing Postcoloniality and Feminism.* Bloomington: Indiana University Press, 1989.

Mirzoeff, Nicholas. "Below the Water: Black Lives Matter and Revolutionary Time." *e-flux journal,* no. 79 (February 2017). https://www.e-flux.com/journal/79/94164/below-the-water-black-lives-matter-and-revolutionary-time/.

Nanni, Giordano. *The Colonisation of Time: Ritual, Routine and Resistance in the British Empire.* Manchester: Manchester University Press, 2009.

Nyong'o, Tavia. "The Crypt of Blackness: or Assotto Saint with Gilles Deleuze." In Gunkel and lynch, *We Travel the Space Ways*, 175–98.

O'Connell, Hugh Charles. "'We Are Change': The Novum as Event in Nnedi Okorafor's *Lagoon*." *Cambridge Journal of Postcolonial Literary Inquiry* 3, no. 3 (2016): 292.

Patterson, Orlando. *Slavery and Social Death: A Comparative Study.* Cambridge, MA: Harvard University Press, 1982.

Prospero, Joseph M. "Saharan Dust Impacts and Climate Change." *Oceanography* 19, no. 2 (2006): 60–61.

Prospero, Joseph M., and Olga L. Mayol-Bracero. "Understanding the Transport and Impact of African Dust on the Caribbean Basin." *Bulletin of the American Meteorological Society* 94, no. 9 (September 2013): 1329–37.

Sharpe, Christina. *In the Wake: On Blackness and Being.* Durham, NC: Duke University Press, 2016.

Smallwood, Stephanie E. *Saltwater Slavery: A Middle Passage from Africa to American Diaspora.* Cambridge, MA: Harvard University Press, 2007.

Steyerl, Hito. "In Free Fall: A Thought Experiment on Vertical Perspective." *e-flux journal*, no. 24 (April 2011). https://www.e-flux.com/journal/24/67860/in-free-fall-a-thought-experiment-on-vertical-perspective/.

Tarkovsky, Andrey. *Sculpting in Time: The Great Russian Filmmaker Discusses His Art.* Translated by Kitty Hunter-Baker. Austin: University of Texas Press, 1989.

Thompson, Krista A. *An Eye for the Tropics: Tourism, Photography, and Framing the Caribbean Picturesque.* Durham, NC: Duke University Press, 2006.

Tremlett, Giles. "After Four Months at Sea, Ghost Ship with 11 Petrified Corpses Washes Up in Barbados." *Guardian*, May 29, 2006. https://www.theguardian.com/world/2006/may/29/gilestremlett.mainsection.

Tsing, Anna Lowenhaupt. "A Feminist Approach to the Anthropocene: Earth Stalked by Man." Helen Pond McIntyre '48 Lecture, Barnard College, New York. Recorded November 10, 2015. Vimeo video, 1:09:52. https://vimeo.com/149475243.

Wilderson, Frank B., III. "The Vengeance of Vertigo: Aphasia and Abjection in the Political Trials of Black Insurgents." *InTensions*, no. 5 (Fall/Winter 2011). http://www.yorku.ca/intent/issue5/articles/frankbwildersoniii.php.

Yusoff, Kathryn. "Geologic Life: Prehistory, Climate, Futures, or Do Fossil Fuels Dream of Geologic Life?" Unpublished manuscript, April 2012. PDF. https://eprints.lancs.ac.uk/id/eprint/73620/1/GeologicLife_April2012_yusoff.pdf.

ACKNOWLEDGMENTS

"Sea Changes and Other Futurisms" started during a journey made possible by a travel grant awarded by the Canada Council for the Arts to attend residencies at Alice Yard in Trinidad and Fresh Milk in Barbados. An earlier version was published by MAP Office in *Our Ocean Guide* (Lightbox Publishing, 2017). Ayesha would also like to thank Taru Elving for the invitation to attend a short residency at the Archipelago Research Institute's field station in Seili, Finland.

Research for "Alien Time" was enabled by a generous fellowship from the Bayreuth Academy of Advanced African Studies. The text was originally published in the anthology *Ghosts, Specters, Revenants* (iwalewabooks, 2020); it appears here with permission. Henriette would like to thank Kitso Lynn Lelliott for making her work accessible for research and for spending so much time sharing her thoughts. Special thanks are also due to Sam Nightingale for his invaluable feedback on an earlier draft of this chapter.

Our conversation is based on a public event at the symposium "Alien Time" held at Goldsmiths in May 2019. Thanks to Bridget Crone for providing that space and to Portia Malatjie for the transcription. We would both like to thank Jorella Andrews for all of her wonderful insights during the preparation of this manuscript.

For all the dislocated time travelers out there imagining other possible futures out of impossible presents. We give thanks.

BIOGRAPHIES

Henriette Gunkel focuses on speculative fiction and the politics of time from a decolonial, queer-feminist perspective. Her most recent publication is the anthology, coedited with kara lynch, *We Travel the Space Ways: Black Imagination, Fragments, and Diffractions* (transcript, 2019). Formerly a lecturer in the Visual Cultures department at Goldsmiths, University of London, she is currently professor at the Institute for Media Studies, Ruhr University Bochum.

Ayesha Hameed's projects *Black Atlantis* and *A Rough History* have been exhibited internationally, including at the biennials in Liverpool (2020), Gothenburg (2019), Lubumbashi (2019), and Dakar (2018). She has contributed to several anthologies, including *Forensis* (Sternberg Press, 2014) and *Unsound/Undead* (Urbanomic, 2019). She is currently a program leader for the PhD in Visual Cultures at Goldsmiths, University of London.

Together with Simon O'Sullivan, Gunkel and Hameed are coeditors of *Futures and Fictions* (Repeater, 2017).

Henriette Gunkel and Ayesha Hameed
VISUAL CULTURES AS **TIME TRAVEL**

Published by Goldsmiths, University of London
and Sternberg Press

Series editor: Jorella Andrews
Managing editor: Max Bach
Copyeditor: Zoë Harris
Proofreading: Sarah Stephenson
Design: Marit Münzberg
Printing: Tallinn Book Printers

Cover image: Full-page miniature by William
de Brailes depicting the flood of Noah
(Genesis 7:11–24), folio 3r, ca. 1250.

ISBN 978-3-95679-538-1

Distributed by The MIT Press, Art Data, and
Les presses du réel

Goldsmiths, University of London
New Cross
UK - London SE14 6NW
www.gold.ac.uk

Sternberg Press
Caroline Schneider
Karl-Marx-Allee 78
D-10243 Berlin
www.sternberg-press.com

Other titles in this series include
VISUAL CULTURES AS **OBJECTS AND AFFECTS**
VISUAL CULTURES AS **RECOLLECTION**
VISUAL CULTURES AS **SERIOUSNESS**
VISUAL CULTURES AS **OPPORTUNITY**